# HEAL
# AND
# MOVE ON

# HEAL AND MOVE ON

Seven steps to recovering from a break-up

ANDREW G. MARSHALL

BLOOMSBURY
LONDON · NEW DELHI · NEW YORK · SYDNEY

*To Hilly Janes*

*Thank you for your support
and showing how to move on with dignity.*

First published in Great Britain 2011

Copyright © 2011 by Andrew G. Marshall

The moral right of the author has been asserted

Some of this material has appeared in a different context in *I Love You But I'm Not In Love With You* and *The Single Trap*, published by Bloomsbury.

Bloomsbury Publishing Plc
50 Bedford Square
London WC1B 3DP

Bloomsbury Publishing, London, New Delhi, New York and Sydney

A CIP catalogue record for this book is available from the British Library

ISBN 978 1 4088 0260 1

10 9 8 7 6 5 4 3 2 1

Typeset by Hewer Text UK Ltd, Edinburgh
Printed and bound in Great Britain by
CPI Group (UK) Ltd, Croydon, CR0 4YY

MIX
Paper from
responsible sources
FSC® C013604

www.bloomsbury.com/andrewgmarshall

# Seven steps to recovering from a break-up

# INTRODUCTION

Seven Steps is a series of books offering straight-forward advice for creating successful and fulfilling relationships. Getting the most out of love needs skills, and the good news is that these skills can be taught. If you have picked up this particular book from the series, your relationship is probably in crisis. My aim is to help you understand how you've got to this point, cope with the panic, discover if your relationship can be salvaged, and deal with the fallout if it can't. More importantly, I want to hold out a promise: it will get better. The worst moment in a crisis is when all the balls are up in the air and the future is an unknowable blank. It is easy to imagine the worst and overlook the opportunities coming over the horizon.

In order to let go of the past and let new things into your life, you need to *heal and move on*. To help you achieve this goal, I have broken the journey down into seven stages with exercises to help you understand yourself better and communicate effectively with your partner. Because there is a lot to absorb, I have put the three key lessons into a nutshell at the end of each chapter. In the dark days, when you feel overwhelmed by the journey, go back and read over the previous step but always remember: *It will get better.*

In writing this book, I have drawn on twenty-five years' experience as a marital therapist working with couples in crisis. I have protected their confidentiality by sometimes merging two or three different cases. In addition, I have used interviews with people not in counselling and letters written to my website. My thanks to everyone who has shared their experiences and made this book possible.

Andrew G. Marshall
www.andrewgmarshall.com

STEP 1

DENIAL

Human beings are not comfortable with change. We want things to stay the same. Nowhere is this instinct more apparent than in our relationships. When we tell our beloved: 'I love you', there is an implicit promise that we'll be there – come what may, for richer for poorer, for ever and ever. So there is nothing sadder than a couple arriving in my counselling room with one claiming 'it's over' and the other hurt, shocked and puzzled but wanting to 'save' the situation. Sometimes it seems that each person has been in a different relationship and neither can understand the other's viewpoint.

If your partner has recently decided that you have no future together, the news can be simply unbelievable. Especially if, like many people in this situation, you have been motoring along reasonably comfortably. There might have been disagreements and attempts to try harder but it seems impossible that things have got this bad. What's more, you have a lovely home, beautiful children and have spent many years together. Sure there are problems, every relationship has problems, but how could it come to this?

If you have recently announced that you want to end years of unhappiness and countless attempts to 'try harder', which went nowhere, it can be frustrating that your partner cannot see that the relationship is broken and that it would be kinder to separate without further heartache. Even if you expected your partner to be upset, the full extent of his or her pain, the pleas for another chance and the angry demands to know why it's over will probably still have left you feeling bewildered. Worse still, no matter how hard you try to explain your decision, nothing seems to get through to your partner.

Therefore this first chapter focuses on helping you understand, or explain, how your relationship reached this point. In my experience, relationships get into trouble for one of *five* main reasons:

## Unsteady Foundations

The moment of falling in love is magical. We can't stop thinking about our beloved, it's like we're walking several inches above the ground and the world seems a far better place. Psychologists call this phenomenon 'limerence' and once under its spell, even our beloved's faults become assets: 'It doesn't matter that she has a temper because I can help her tame it' or 'So what if he drinks because I can save him from himself.'

Under normal circumstances, obstacles – like living great distances apart – would be a serious problem. Under limerence, they become just another chance to prove our love. I have coun-selled couples who met while one was on the run from the law and others where one partner was a heroin addict. All their friends felt that the chance of long-term success for these relationships was slim to zero. However, under the spell of limer-ence, love is literally blind and these couples ploughed on regardless.

Unfortunately, limerence does not last for ever – normally about eighteen months to three years. Once its effect wears off, reality begins to intrude. A good example is James and Cathy, who met when they were recipients of organ transplants from the same man. Cathy had lived a very sheltered life: 'Even as a child I'd needed regular kidney dialysis and whenever I asked to go somewhere or do some-thing my parents would say: "I don't think that's a good idea." But I never minded too much because they made up for my handicap in other ways.'

When she came for counselling, she reminded me of a china doll – even though she was nearly thirty. James was a complete contrast; he was slightly older, more confident and a bit of a Jack the Lad: 'I take life as I find it.' In hospital, they had spent time recovering together and their unique bond quickly developed into love. Cathy's parents violently disapproved. James was not 'good enough' for their 'Princess', but Cathy was enjoying her freedom and took no notice.

Once limerence began to wane, the couple seemed almost comically different. James would come home and relax on the sofa in his dirty work overalls – which was abhorrent to Cathy, whose father worked in a clean office but still had a shower and changed when he arrived home (in case he'd brought any germs into the house). Their rows were particularly destructive because under the influence of limerence, they had never really argued before; they had instead distracted themselves by leaping into bed.

Couples who make the transition from limerence to long-term love learn how to argue effectively and negotiate a way through their differences. Over time, they develop confidence in the 'rightness' of their relationship by surviving crises together and developing a multifaceted bond. This is a real resource on which to build a future. Unfortunately, limerence can bind mismatched couples – like Cathy and James – who wake up and realise they have major problems and nothing to fall back on but fantasies of how life could be together and the memories of the crazy part of falling in love. This scenario is particularly painful when one partner comes out of limerence before the other, realises that he or she has made a mistake, and their boyfriend or girlfriend is still deep under its influence.

## Final Straws

These couples have had long-lasting relation-ships but the bond has weakened over time and seems more based on habit than love. The children get off to school at the right time, there is food on the table and the house is clean, but there is very little joy. Sometimes one partner can be very controlling and the other feels that he or she cannot truly be themselves if the other is around.

Whatever the circumstances, the couples develop a 'his and hers' vision of the marriage. Often one partner will be happy enough, enjoying the quiet life and comforts of being one half of a relationship. These people have low expectations but at least they are met. In contrast, the other partner is living a life of quiet desperation. 'I looked round my kitchen. I'd just folded the tea towels and watered my pots of herbs growing on the windowsill and thought: "There's got to be more to life than this",' said Martha, thirty-five. 'Philip doesn't like spicy food so I have to smuggle my herbs into my cooking. He seems happy enough with the same old, same old but I want to see the world. I want to have some fun.' She tried on many occasions to discuss her feelings but Philip was happy staying at home.

When the crisis point comes for this kind of relationship, it is very seldom dramatic. 'I'd come back from the supermarket and I was surrounded by half-empty shopping bags. Philip walked into the kitchen. He nodded. He might have grunted but he certainly didn't talk to me. He just made himself a cup of tea and took it upstairs. I stared at the unpacked shopping and thought: "If he can't even say hello or offer me a cup of tea, what's the point?" It was like a blinding flash of clarity in a life of greyness.' When Martha announced she wanted a divorce, Philip was stunned. 'We get on, we have a lovely house, two great children. Isn't that enough?' He offered to make hundreds of cups of tea and he researched a holiday in Venice, but no matter what Philip promised, Martha remained adamant. It had been the final straw. Her underlying vision of the relationship had switched from good enough to broken and their 'his and hers' philosophies of marriage could no longer be reconciled.

## Train Track Relationships

These couples work very well as a team. Each partner has their separate sphere: normally he is a successful businessman and she has brought up the children. Their lives run along parallel but separate tracks with little or no crossover. He does not talk about his work and she makes the decisions about the children alone because he's away and does not understand the intricacies of the family timetable. They often have a good social life – revolving around the family or other couples

– but spend little or no time together. Even if they did once have things in common, their central relationship as lovers has been replaced by joint parenting. There is no friction because either they seldom have meaningful conversations or they have traded control in one area (for instance, how money is spent) for no influence in the other (such as what's happening this weekend).

A typical example would be Adam and Jenny who were in their mid-forties but had known each other since college: 'We want different things. I'm very sporty and go potholing and take walking holidays. Jenny is more "book on the beach". That bores me stupid; I'd have to go waterskiing and it's not so much fun on your own. When the boys were younger they joined me, but nowadays they're not so keen on holidaying with Mum and Dad.'

Train track relationships are often derailed when the eldest child leaves home. In fact, the most common problem that first-year students bring to university counselling services is their parents' sudden and inexplicable divorce. Without the glue of children and the distraction of their demands, couples wake up and realise that they are strangers. This can be an opportunity to rediscover each other but train track partnerships often fall foul of either one or both of the next two reasons.

## Mid-life Revolution

Although everyone knows our time on earth is limited, when we're young it is possible to imagine life stretching into the blue yonder. However, somewhere in our middle years, we have to face reality. Sometimes the death of a parent will focus our mind, sometimes redundancy or boredom at work. Whatever the cause, we realise: 'I have only thirty or forty years left' or 'I've still got enough time to train for what I really want to do' or 'I've got to stop wasting my life.' Hopefully, our partner is sympathetic and supports our desire to change. However, sometimes the person gripped by a mid-life revolution cannot explain their sudden desire to, for example, form a rock band and perform in local pubs and their partner may laugh at the idea.

Other people undergoing their mid-life revolution have partners who are quite happy with their lives, thank you, and don't want them turned upside down. So a gap between the couple opens up and, over time, it widens into an unbridgeable abyss. Alternatively, the person undergoing the mid-life revolution will wake up and think: 'I'm still attractive enough to meet someone else.'

Adam found himself in exactly this plight: 'I really like Jenny. I want the best for her, but I don't want to spend the rest of my life with her. At the moment, we're both still young enough to find someone who will suit us better.'

Another version of the mid-life revolution will be someone who suddenly wants children but their partner is either unable or unwilling to oblige. 'I felt terrible leaving, especially after the second round of infertility treatment failed,' says Marcus who is forty-two. 'My girlfriend decided that she didn't want a third go and something inside me died. Up to that moment, I never realised how important being a dad was to me.' Within weeks, he had announced that he had fallen out of love, moved out, and started dating a work colleague.

## Unforgivable Betrayal

If a couple can communicate well, and all the problems are on the table, no matter how terrible the situation is, most people can muddle through. However, secrets and lies are nearly always fatal to a relationship. For example, Lydia and Jeremy divorced after she discovered that he'd had a vasectomy before they got married but had not told her. 'What made it doubly difficult was that we had discussed children at the outset, and he had sat back silently while I went for all sorts of invasive tests – all the time knowing the reason why I wasn't getting pregnant,' she explained.

Affairs are also built on secrets and lies and although I can help most couples recover and build a stronger and better relationship – I go into this in detail in my book *How Can I Ever Trust You Again?* published by Bloomsbury – there is one category of infidelity that often proves to be unforgivable.

'I was devastated when I discovered that my wife had been having an affair. I've known her for fifteen years and it turned romantic about eight years ago. We have a toddler whom we both love dearly,' Frederick posted on my website. 'We have now attended five relationship therapy sessions and she has not been forthcoming about the affair until recently, when she told me that it started about a year or so ago. Although she confirms at every session that she wants to give our relationship another go – three months after stopping contact with her lover – she continues to have surprisingly strong feelings for him and her love for me is not returning. She says that if she could, she would "flick a switch" and make things better.'

Frederick found it increasingly hard to live in limbo while his wife made up her mind and suggested a temporary separation. However, worse was to come and later he wrote again: 'I've just found out that she has continued to have contact with her lover and she has lied to both me and our therapist for the last thirteen sessions! It's time to call it quits – for my sake – as she seems unable to see what she's doing and that her view of love is simply a fantasy.'

Not all betrayals are of a romantic nature but the sense of trust being violated is very similar. 'I always knew that Jim had a gambling problem – and in our younger days we'd had to move a couple of times in a hurry – but his business was successful and finally we bought a lovely house,' said Allison. 'I put my heart and soul into that place and so I was devastated when we had to sell because of more stupid gambling debts.' Jim was more pragmatic: 'It was only a house, we've still got each other.' Unfortunately, something inside Allison had snapped: 'I thought I could forgive but when the removal van arrived outside the place that we're renting – and it's not that bad – I knew I could never trust him again.' Although they had been married for over twenty years, and had two children and lots of good memories, it soon became clear that their marriage was over.

A common cause of feeling betrayed is an abortion. Although the couple may decide to seek the termination together, one partner (normally the woman) feels under so much pressure that there seems no alternative but to go along with the idea. Normally the relationship continues for some time after the termination but the unresolved issues leave a scar that does not heal. 'I kept expecting him to come through the clinic door and stop it,' said Gemma. It took a further six years before they arrived in my counselling room but the termination proved an insurmountable obstacle to solving their relationship problems.

## LOOK BACK WITH FRESH EYES

If you still cannot understand why your relationship is in crisis, try this exercise:

1. If you were pushed to come up with a time when things started to go wrong, when would that be?

2. Find some time when you won't be interrupted and take a pen and piece of paper, sit down, and close your eyes.

3. Imagine yourself back at the time your relationship took a wrong turn and let the movie of your life play out from that point. Watch what your partner does. Look at what you do.

4. Whenever you come to something in the movie where you feel uncomfortable, open your eyes and jot down a few notes.

5. Return to the movie and keep going until you hit another difficult moment. Write down the details.

6. Watch the movie until you reach the present day.

7. Look over your notes and review them. What new information have you learned? What would you like to change?

8. Discuss your findings with your partner.

## Denial and the Break-up of Relationships

One of the main reasons why it is so hard to accept that a relationship has ended is the gap between a problem arising and it becoming fatal.

This is illustrated by a long-term study into why relationships fail. Social scientists Paul Amato and Stacy J. Rogers surveyed over two thousand married people in the US and asked them, 'Have you had a problem because one of you: a) gets angry easily; b) has feelings which are easily hurt; c) gets jealous; d) is domineering; e) is critical; f) gets moody; g) won't talk; h) has been unfaithful; i) has irritating habits; j) is not home enough; k) spends money foolishly; l) has problems with drink or drugs?' They asked the same questions at regular intervals over the next twelve years and checked on everybody's marital status. The most common reasons for divorce were:

1. Infidelity
2. Spending money foolishly
3. Drinking and drugs
4. Jealousy
5. Irritating habits
6. Moodiness

However, most of the people who would go on to split up had reported a high number of problems as early as nine to twelve years prior to their divorce. So why the big time lag? In every relationship, there is normally one partner who will raise issues (and talk them through) and one who seeks to contain problems (and keep a sense of proportion). Both roles are equally important and valuable. Unfortunately, when problems mount up, the partner who raises issues will naturally want to talk more and more. The partner who seeks to contain problems will naturally try harder and harder to keep a lid on things. The result is that the couple become stuck and the problems become more and more ingrained. In an ideal world, this would be the point when they would seek professional help. Unfortunately, many people choose to close their eyes to the full extent of their problems. This is why I have called the first stage Denial.

Both partners keep their heads down, hope that something will change or that Christmas, a holiday, renovating the house or starting a new job will make things better. In the short term, circumstances will shift for the better or one of these minor changes will help. However, what normally happens is that the 'raiser' of the issues gives up and stops trying to talk about the problems. After all, it has got him or her nowhere. The 'container' will actually feel better as their partner appears not to be so 'picky', 'nagging' or 'critical'. So they are doubly shocked when the raiser suddenly announces that the relationship is over. At this moment, the raiser turns into the *leaver* (who wants to separate) and the container into the *sticker* (who wants to save the relationship).

When I first met Donald, forty-five, he was angry, resentful and couldn't comprehend why his wife of twenty-five years wanted to leave him. 'My wife has sent me "to sort myself out". She keeps telling me "it's over" and to "get used to the idea" but how can it be?' he explained at his first solo session. 'She just wants to give up, after all we've been through together. I've worked hard and we've got a nice house, very few debts and five children. Surely we owe it to them to give it another try.'

I asked Donald to take me through the history of his marriage. His job involved long and unsociable hours and his wife had raised the children basically single-handed. 'I always thought we were happy in our own fields and as I got more established and the children grew up, we'd spend more time together.' Donald was very matter of fact in my counselling office and it was difficult to see the pain hidden behind the determination to stick at his marriage.

A few weeks later, I invited his wife, Deborah, to come for a solo session. The contrast between them could not have been more marked. Over the past few years, she had trained and qualified for a new job helping the disabled and had done a lot of personal growth. 'I was unhappy for a long time and there have been lots of times that Donald let me down – but that's in the past. I've moved on,' she explained. It was clear that they had both spent a lot of time in denial. 'We went out for a Valentine's Day meal several years ago and we just sat across the table and looked at each other. We had nothing whatsoever to talk about. After that, we'd go out with other couples as that avoided the difficult silences.' Although Deborah had subsequently broken through her denial, Donald was still deeply imbedded. As he later admitted: 'I was like a zombie. Not thinking. Not living. Just working. Totally detached from my feelings.' Fortunately, Donald was brave enough to stick with his counselling and work through the next six stages. However, many people get stuck in denial and become depressed.

## ARE YOU CLINICALLY DEPRESSED?

Depression is hard to diagnose, because everybody gets the blues from time to time. Answering yes to five or more of the following can indicate a serious depression:

- Are you eating too much or too little?
- Do you find it hard to sleep, or sleep too much?
- Do you feel tired all the time or generally lacking energy?
- Do you feel inadequate?
- Are you less productive than you used to be at home or at work?
- Do you have trouble concentrating or making decisions?
- Do you have a tendency to brood over things, feel sorry for yourself or be pessimistic about the future?
- Does the world seem grey?
- Are you easily irritated?
- Do you rarely enjoy or feel interested in pleasurable activities?
- Are you prone to crying?

Anyone recognising two or more symptoms should also speak to their doctor; especially if the symptoms have existed more or less constantly, with no more than a couple of months' relief, for two or more years. Other suggestions for dealing with depression include consulting a nutritionist to check on diet, cutting down on alcohol consumption and taking more exercise – as an aerobic-style workout releases endorphins, the body's natural feel-good hormone.

# Summing Up

Couples can be in denial about the true state of their relationship for years. However, it is very seldom that both partners open their eyes at the same time or as wide as each other: usually one half initiates talks about splitting up – whom I call the Leaver – while the other resists – the Sticker. As each side of this divide views the situation completely differently, I have split my advice into two boxes.

> ## NUTSHELLS FOR LEAVERS:
> - Be aware that your partner is still in denial and will need time to catch up.
> - Remember that change is frightening and it will be easier for your partner if you don't rush headlong into the future.
> - Try and keep an open mind.

**NUTSHELLS FOR STICKERS:**

- You are embarking on a tough journey, so remember to look after yourself and seek out sources of support.
- Be patient with your partner if he or she cannot give a clear or understandable reason for leaving. It takes a multitude of interlocking issues to reach such a decision.
- If your relationship has been in a rut, try a different approach. If you have shut down, try asking questions. If you have talked over your partner or changed the subject, try listening.

STEP 2

CRISIS

'It was like I was strolling along a quiet street on a sunny summer's afternoon; a nice neighbourhood with well-tended lawns, kids playing and men washing cars. When, out of nowhere, a car came hurtling round the corner, mounted the pavement and knocked me down. As it flipped me in the air and my face hit the tarmac, I noticed that my husband was driving the car. Why was he doing this to me?'

This is how Margaret, who had been married for seventeen years, described the impact of hearing her husband confess that he was unhappy and wanted to leave. Just like in a car crash, she felt disorientated, confused and very frightened. She kept thinking: 'There must be some mistake' and 'What do I do now?' But, unlike a road traffic accident, there was no ambulance on the way and nobody to offer a cup of sugary tea.

Shock is a natural reaction to a crisis. The Sticker will need time for the news to sink in – even if the relationship has been unhappy for several years – and sometimes will have to go over the same information several times. In theory, there should be less shock for the Leaver – after all, he or she has initiated the conversation. However, it is impossible to predict how your partner will react. 'I sort of expected him to shrug and take it on the chin,' said Susanna, forty-three, 'but he went into overdrive. He spoke to my mother, my friends and booked a counselling session. I'd been so used to him walking away whenever I tried to talk that it came as a complete surprise that he actually cared.' When the shock wore off, Susanna was actually rather angry about her partner's reaction: 'Why couldn't he have listened before? Why did he wait until my hand was on the door?'

Sometimes when the Leaver announces their decision to end the relationship, their partner can be very matter of fact or quiet. Many Leavers are relieved and think, 'That didn't go badly.' However, this is possibly one of the worst reactions. I call these people 'Silent Stickers' because they want the relationship to continue but are either unable (because expressing emotions is out of character) or unwilling (for fear of losing face) to fight back. These are the partners who are uncooperative, pick fights over incidental matters and hire aggressive legal advisers.

## Unhelpful Coping Strategies for Stickers

Once the shock of the crisis has begun to ease, the partner who wants to save the relationship will fall into one or more of the following four traps:

### Minimising

Some people deal with unwelcome news by dismissing or downplaying it. Using this mindset, they tell themselves that the Leaver does not mean what he or she says or is exaggerating the problem. Alternatively, they believe that the Leaver might be 'ill' or 'going through a difficult time'. Therefore, the Sticker keeps his or her head down and hopes the problem will go away. Although I have counselled female Stickers who use this strategy, it is overwhelmingly a male phenomenon. In Amato and Rogers' research, they discovered that men reported fewer marital problems than women. Although the men listed their own failings, they were less likely to mention their wives' contributions to the marital problems – especially those related to emotions (such as anger, moodiness or being easily hurt). In contrast, the women appeared equally aware of both their own and their husband's failings.

'It sounds weird when I say it now but my wife would do the "feelings" bit of our relationship,' says Christopher, thirty-two. 'She would not only decide the best way to approach our daughter about difficult things – such as wanting to attend an all-night party – but would also remind me to go and visit my mother. I just buried myself at work.' So when she announced it was over, he felt like 'a ship at sea without a rudder, trying to understand but completely out of control'. To continue the analogy, he battened down the hatches and minimised. He consulted his doctor and came back with an offer of tranquillisers and anti-depressants for his wife. When she did nothing about leaving, he thought the worst had 'blown over'. So he had a terrible shock when a letter arrived from her solicitor.

**Breakthrough tip:** Instead of trying to talk your partner round, really listen to them. Instead of using the time when they're talking to think of ways to knock down their arguments, hear what is being said. Instead of looking for solutions, understand your partner's viewpoint by asking questions: How long have you felt like that? What made you think that? How have I made things worse? Keep listening and then listen just a little bit more. When you think that you've got the full picture, repeat back your findings to your partner and check they are correct. If you give your partner the compliment of attentive listening, he or she will return the favour and listen to your opinions too. Finally, the two of you can have an informed debate about the future.

## Repetition

Instead of responding to what the Leaver is saying, the Sticker repeats the same message over and over. Occasionally, he or she will rephrase or restate their case but never engages with the Leaver's feelings or problems. Donald, whom we met in the previous chapter, had a narrow repertoire of responses to his wife Deborah: 'It's not fair', 'It's so hard', 'I can't see why we can't give it another try' and 'I need more time'. When the couple had their first joint counselling session, I discovered just how unproductive this strategy had become. Deborah was tired of dealing with the same questions and statements. So she had started stonewalling back: 'You know why', 'I've told you that before' or 'This is getting us nowhere'. When I stepped in to break the deadlock, she explained: 'There's no point saying anything more because we just have the same old arguments. I've moved on and now Donald needs to do the same.' The other major problem with repetition, just like minimising, is that the Leaver thinks the Sticker is not only refusing to listen but also does not accept the gravity of the crisis.

**Breakthrough tip:** Instead of blaming your partner, take your share of the responsibility. What have you done that has contributed to the problems? Which of your partner's complaints are justified? If you were given a second chance, what would you do differently? Next make a full apology. This has three parts: a) what you regret, b) an acknowledgement of the impact of your behaviour and c) a commitment to change. For example: a) 'I apologise for not listening.' b) 'I realise that this made you feel belittled.' c) 'I've decided not to jump in or shout when I hear something that I don't like.' Do not give explanations or mitigating circumstances. The first invites an argument and the second dilutes the power of the apology.

## Rationalising

This strategy is an improvement over the previous ones, as at least the Sticker is listening and engaging with the Leaver. Unfortunately, the Sticker is engaging only with facts and trying to debate their way out of the crisis. The result is that he or she comes across as rather detached – the last message to give someone with one foot out of the relationship. Donald would often alternate between repetition and rationalising: 'It's really hard on the kids. I don't think Deborah's thought through the impact of family breakdown and she's really left them to fend for themselves lately while she's been out pursuing her career.' Unfortunately, this approach invites a similarly rational response and Deborah told him: 'You're exaggerating. The schools are set up to help them and it's not like they're the only ones who go through this sort of thing.' In this way, she did not need to engage with his feelings of hurt, pain and betrayal. Worse still, she would counter complain: 'Why are you suddenly so concerned about the children? When was the last time you did anything for them?'

**Breakthrough tip:** There are three elements to making a successful case. The first is logic (which you have already mastered). The second, however, is engaging with your emotions. How do you feel? What lurks behind your anger? To get a better understanding of your emotions, keep a feelings diary and write down not only what happened but what you felt. Don't forget to put down the tender and positive emotions as well as the painful and difficult ones. This will help you communicate better with your partner. The third element for a successful case is backing up your words with actions. Instead of just talking about his concerns for the children's welfare, Donald took his youngest son to the dentist when his wife was busy (and thereby also showed that he supported her new career).

## Catastrophising

When bad things happen, we generally roll up our sleeves, clean up the mess and try and make the best of things. However, sometimes the situation seems so bleak that these coping mechanisms are overwhelmed. In most cases, this is because someone has turned a drama into a catastrophe. A good example would be Maria, fifty-two, whose husband had an affair and, although he ended it, decided that his marriage was over too: 'He has completely ruined my life and the children's. We will never get over this. Nobody wants a woman my age. I'll be on my own for ever.' The enormity of her problems had made her shut down totally and, like many people who catastrophise, she had minimised her husband's unhappiness ('Life isn't all rides on merry-go-rounds, we just have to get on with it') and used repetition ('I meant my marriage vows. It is obvious that he didn't') and threats ('Wait till the children find out just what sort of man their father is'). Whenever it seemed that Maria was beginning to cope, a voice would start up in her head, forecasting doom and disaster until she was completely paralysed by fear.

**Breakthrough tip:** Instead of letting negative thoughts turn an unhappy situation into a catastrophe, put up a mental stop signal and get out a piece of paper. Across the top write: 'If we split up . . .' and then underneath write down all the implications. When you have finished writing down all your fears, go back and challenge your conclusions. Have you exaggerated? What evidence is there for these claims? For example, when I challenged Maria about exaggeration she admitted: 'OK, we won't *never* get over this, but it will take a long time.' How long? 'Two or three years, perhaps a little bit more.' Instead of being a catastrophe, the divorce had become something (admittedly still horrible) that ultimately she could survive. When I challenged her about the evidence for 'ruining the children's lives', Maria admitted: 'They're grown-up, with established lives of their own. I suppose I don't know what will happen because I don't have a crystal ball.' The divorce was still sad but no longer a catastrophe and Maria was able to move forward.

## EVEN SPLIT EXERCISE

Take a piece of paper and draw a line down the middle. On one side write 'My responsibility' and on the other 'His [or her] responsibility'.

1. Start with your partner's side – as this is normally the easiest – and list all his or her contributing factors for the break-up.
2. Next list your contributing factors for the break-up on your side of the paper.
3. Finally, compare both sets of responsibilities. Are they linked in any way? Could your behaviour have prompted a matching response from your partner? For example: 'He always pushed

for more sex' could prompt 'I used sex as a weapon to get my own back on him.'

4.  If you find it very hard to think of anything for one particular column, ask a friend to help and make suggestions.

## Can We Save This Relationship?

Once the shock has worn off and all the unhappiness is out in the open, both the Leaver and the Sticker need to reassess. For the Leaver, your honesty could have triggered a corresponding honesty from your partner and a willingness finally to face the problems. Many people find themselves asking: could we have a future together after all? For the Sticker, you have a clearer understanding of your partner's position and although your goal might still be to save the relationship, it is important to be realistic. Fighting against the odds is hard enough but fighting a losing battle is demoralising, draining and, ultimately, pointless.

Whether you are the Leaver or the Sticker, look at the following factors and total up how many blight your relationship:

1. There is no shared humour.
2. It is extremely difficult to show affection.
3. My heart sinks as I head home because I've no idea what to expect when I arrive.
4. It feels like I'm walking on eggshells.
5. There are put-downs, and there is name-calling and aggressive body language (like eye rolling, deep sighs and walking away).
6. Any attempt to discuss the problems turns into blaming and making excuses.
7. I feel victimised.
8. My partner seems both hostile and detached.
9. Anything I say is given the worst spin until I'm frightened to open my mouth.
10. My partner is resigned and says things like 'whatever', 'do what you please' and 'I'm too tired to fight.'

## How to analyse the results

**Up to four:** Although the picture is gloomy, there is still enough goodwill to build a future. Be grateful that your relationship has not succumbed to some of the most destructive kinds of behaviour. Read some of the other titles in this series, such as: *Build a Life-long Love Affair*, *Resolve Your Differences* or *Help Your Partner Say 'Yes'*.

**Five to seven:** When we are angry and disappointed, it is easy to start taking out our unhappiness on our partner. We tell ourselves that our bad behaviour is justified by their bad behaviour. Unfortunately, our partner is making the same justifications and we become trapped in a downward spiral. So look at the exercise again and ask yourself: How many times have I been guilty of these negative behaviours myself? What could I change? If these questions help you to look at yourself through different eyes, it is likely that there is still hope for your relationship. If, however, they make you angry or defensive, your relationship is probably beyond saving.

**Eight and over:** Your home is a very unhappy place at the moment. There seems to be little constructive communication between you and your partner. Ultimately, it takes two people to make a relationship and it doesn't look as though there is enough goodwill or trust for you to work together.

## FRIGHTENED OF CHANGE?

If your partner is talking about new goals and ambitions, the changes involved can feel pretty scary. If you want to change, but are worried how your partner will react, this can also feel scary. Either way, here are the three keys to coping with change:

1.  **Understanding**

    Change is neither intrinsically good nor bad; it is all down to how you look at it. For example, we think of rain as bad but in a desert rain would be wonderful. It depends on our attitude. So the first step is always to look for the upside of something new. If you can't see one immediately, try looking a bit further into the future. How might it look in three months' time, a year, two years? Secondly, ask what would happen if you didn't change? What is the downside of staying where you are?

2.  **Relax**

    Scientists have discovered that when we're under stress – like at times of change – our brain operates differently. With our very survival under threat, we use the less sophisticated parts of our brain inherited from our reptile ancestors. Yet this is the very time that we need to think something through, rather than just act instinctively. So next time you're stressed by change, find a way to relax and calm down. For example, take deep breaths, go for a long walk, dig the garden or spring-clean the house. Later, think back to times when you successfully dealt with change – there will be plenty of examples as you're better at coping than you think. Now look at what worked last time and what skills can be used today.

3. **Name your fears**

When you are relaxed, close your eyes and picture the proposed future. Where will it be? What will it be like? What will your partner be doing? Make the picture as detailed as possible. Next try and analyse what is particularly worrying. Write each of these fears down in a sentence. Go back to the picture and try and imagine other things that could be unsettling you. Write these down too. It is better to have a list of fears on a piece of paper – however long – than a large amorphous terror in your head. Go back to the list and cross off anything that, on reflection, is a molehill rather than a mountain. Finally discuss your fears with your partner. He or she might be able to offer reassurance or provide more information to take the edge off your anxiety. Even if some fears remain, you will have a clearer grasp of the most important issues.

# What If My Partner Will Not Accept that the Relationship is Over?

There comes a time when splitting up is the best option. Trying to talk about the problems just goes round in ever-decreasing circles or pumps up the anger and pain. It should be clear that the relationship is over. However, when you explain your decision to your partner, he or she just does not seem to hear. So what's going on? In most cases, I discover that the partner who wants to leave is giving mixed messages. The following seven steps are designed to help you communicate simply, effectively and with the least amount of pain.

## Step 1: Get off the roller coaster

All the arguing, defending and explaining that come with a disintegrating relationship can really get the adrenaline going. The lows might be terrible, but the highs – when your partner thinks he or she is getting their message across – are incredible. Worse still, your partner has probably reached the point where even negative attention – tears, shouting and name-calling – is better than nothing. So get off the roller coaster and respond to invitations to fight or pleadings in a neutral manner: 'I'm too tired' or 'I'm too stressed' or 'I've had enough'. Use this time out to check that you really want to end the relationship.

## Step 2: Communicate

Once the temperature in the house has normalised a little, you are ready to talk. The important thing to remember is: keep it simple. In fact, one sentence is enough. For example, 'I don't think our relationship has got a future and I'm planning to move out.' If you try and justify your choice, it will just start another ride on the roller coaster. So stick to the facts and your central message. If this seems difficult, you might like to write your sentence down and refine it first.

## Step 3: Do not try and soften the blow

Words and phrases like 'maybe' or 'someday' or 'in the future' or 'who knows' might seem kinder. However, what you see as letting your partner down gently will be seized on and fuel his or her hopes for a future together with you. You might need to repeat the message as it takes a while for bad news to sink in. If your partner is in shock, it might have to be on another day.

## Step 4: Respond to flowers, texts and notes politely but restate your message

When the entreaties come, do not ignore them. Your partner will be putting all his or her hopes on this magic bullet. So it is cruel to leave them hanging and wondering about your response. Instead, say 'thank you' and repeat your sentence again.

## Step 5: The follow-up

By now, your partner will begin to think that you might really want to end the relationship. He or she will be desperate to talk and plead for the last time. Once again, it would be cruel to refuse. Set up a rendezvous somewhere neutral – with no past associations – and fix it for a few days into the future. This will give your partner a while to focus on his or her message and for you to think and be certain too.

## Step 6: Really listen

Let your partner talk and do not interrupt. When he or she has made their pitch, ask questions: 'How would we do that?' or seek clarification: 'Why do you feel that way?' Do not respond or explain your position, just encourage your partner to keep talking until all his or her hopes and fears are out in the open. If you offer this courtesy, your partner is likely to offer the same to you. Hopefully, it will become clear that your two versions of the future are incompatible.

## Step 7: Check whether your subsequent behaviour could be misinterpreted

There could be times when you might have contact. For example, his mother has invited you to her birthday party and he will be there too; her daughter from a previous marriage is getting married and wants you there too. Whatever the circumstances, put yourself in your partner's shoes. How could someone who wants to get back together with you interpret your actions? If there's a risk of you being misinterpreted, explain your position to your partner in advance. At the event itself, keep your communication polite, short and sweet.

## What If My Partner is Slipping Away?

The first option is to try and communicate in a different way.

- If you normally talk face to face, write a letter.
- Alternatively, fewer words can be more powerful than lots, especially if you are someone who would normally write an eight-page letter. Buying a greetings card, sending a text or scrawling a message in lipstick on the mirror could make your partner take notice.
- If you do not talk intimately on the phone or seldom email each other, these are other options.
- In other words, anything that will surprise your partner, stop them from thinking 'same old, same old' and switching off.

If the above fails, step back and stop chasing.

- Take a deep breath and reassess your relationship.
- Have you been so busy looking for solutions

– like a holiday away – that you have not truly listened to your partner?

- Sometimes when the Sticker stops taking all the responsibility for saving the relationship, the Leaver has enough space to stop running and reassess.

- Be realistic. Although a study in the *Journal of Marriage and Family* in 2003 found a third of couples who break up get back together, these tend to be those in more established relationships (with children and joint mortgages). When the study looked at the relationships of people under thirty, the reunion rate dropped to just one in ten.

## Summing Up

During a crisis, it is common for one or both partners to go into shock. It is particularly easy for Stickers to shut down and retreat into behaviour which helps them cope with the enormity of events but which pushes Leavers further out the door. However, it is helpful for both partners to take another look at whether the relationship can still be saved; even if it proves to be a lost cause, this process will make the eventual split more of a joint decision and therefore less fraught.

## NUTSHELLS FOR LEAVERS:

- Use this opportunity to re-examine your relationship and be certain about your choice.
- Recognise any positive changes made by your partner, as this will encourage long-term cooperation – vital if you have children together.
- Give clear and consistent messages to your partner.

## NUTSHELLS FOR STICKERS:

- Don't put all the blame for your relationship's breakdown on your partner. Although he or she might have fired the starting pistol, this is not the whole picture.
- Look at your own behaviour and take your share of responsibility for the crisis.
- Listen to what your partner is saying and imagine, for a moment, that his or her feelings are valid. What would you say? How would you change your behaviour?

STEP 3

# ADJUSTMENT

Once the denial and shock has worn off, and both the Sticker and the Leaver begin to process the impact of the crisis, it soon becomes clear that the reasons for the relationship breaking down and the implications are more complex than either partner first imagined. Previously, the fact that the relationship has collapsed has been under a micro-scope – sometimes to the exclusion of everything else. In the third stage, Adjustment, the camera pulls slowly back from the fracture and shows the bigger picture. Although the information revealed is different for the Sticker and the Leaver, the process is the same. The Leaver discovers that just announcing the end of the relationship does not solve all the problems – but actually presents a new set of obstacles to negotiate. The Sticker stops simply blaming the Leaver and begins to take his or her share of the responsibility, understand the depth of the problems and starts to consider the fundamental changes needed to save the relationship.

## Questions for Stickers

By answering these questions as fully as possible, you will begin to adjust your view of the problems and either find a way to save your relationship or put down the foundations for healing and moving on.

### How did I get to here?

When I work with people whose partners are threatening to leave or have left, I find it is useful to go back to their first significant relationship: with their parents. These early experiences set the template for the rest of our lives.

Donald, whom we met previously, was the youngest of seven children. Life was hard for his mother not only because she had so many children but also because money was tight. Her husband was a labourer and drank a large proportion of his wages. I asked Donald: what was it like growing up in that household? 'I think this might be why I've been so driven to get away and prove myself,' said Donald.

There were also clues about why he was so shut off from his feelings. 'Not only was it hard to be heard – with so many people in the house – but also Dad was either at work or in the pub and Mum was so busy. I suppose I didn't talk much because nobody listened.' I asked him to think about a strong memory from his childhood which might sum up his experiences: 'I must have been about five and Mum had to go out to work, so Dad took me to a childminder. I think she might have been a second cousin or something but for some reason I didn't like her. I climbed on to my little toy tractor and pedalled round to the school where I knew I'd find my older brothers and sisters.' He stopped for a moment. 'I haven't thought about that in years.' 'So what does it tell you?' I asked. 'If there's a problem I run away. Even today, if we're about to have a row, I get in the car and go for a drive.' 'Or bury yourself in work?' I prompted and Donald nodded.

Turning now to your own situation, think about how you got to this point. Look at some old family pictures or watch home movies. What story could you tell? Maybe write it down or imagine it in detail. What light does this episode shed on your dilemma today?

## What do I want from my relationship?

When we have been with a partner for a while, our relationship becomes a given part of our lives. So we never really stop and ask: is this the sort of relationship that I've always wanted? Sophie is fifty-three and fighting to keep her husband – a high-powered businessman whose work involves a lot of travel.

'We've lived abroad for large chunks of time and although the sunshine lifestyle has a lot to recommend it, the ex-pat communities are often very inward-looking and gossipy. Even today with cheaper flights, it means a lot of time away from my extended family and friends. So I've made a lot of sacrifices.'

I asked Sophie to make a list of all the qualities that she brought to the relationship down one side of the page and, down the other side, all the things that she needed from a relationship. Down her side, she put loyalty, commitment, honesty, good mother, etc. She found it hard to think about what she needed: 'I've never really thought about it before. I suppose that's really revealing.'

However, I persisted and she wrote: Togetherness, consideration, laughter. Did her marriage provide these things? 'It seems like it's always me having to compromise and to be honest, there hasn't been much emphasis on my needs at all.'

Try this exercise for yourself. What do you bring to your relationship? What do you want/ need? With many of my clients, there is a big gulf between what someone needs and what their partner offers. It is almost as if these Stickers are not fighting to be with their particular partner but, rather, to stay married.

## What do I want to change about my life?

If anything positive has come out of this journey so far, it has been a wake-up call. Instead of plodding along, unquestioning, making it through the daily grind, step back and look not just at your relationship but at everything. 'Talking about my childhood, I've realised that I never really knew my father,' said Donald. 'I would hate to be a stranger to my children because I've been so busy earning to keep a roof over our heads rather than living in it.' So I asked what *one* change he could make that would kick-start this process. He decided to talk to his eldest son – whom he felt was a bit adrift in the world – and tell him how much he loved him. It proved to be a very emotional experience and Donald cried. However, he did not run away – as he might have done in the past – and learned a lot about himself and his son: 'He said he knew that I loved him and he'd always felt that I was there for him.'

Turning again to your situation, what changes would you like to make to your relationship with your parents, children or friends? What about work? What are your ambitions for the future?

## Questions for Leavers

By answering these questions as fully as possible, you will begin to adjust your view of your relationship, be 100 per cent certain that you are making the right decision and, if you are, lay the foundations for your new life.

### How did I get to here?

Look back over your relationship and think about the moments when it took a turn for the worse. What was your contribution? How much responsibility should you take for the poor communication? Sometimes with your partner putting all the blame on you for wanting to end the relationship, it is easy to become defensive and close your eyes to any personal mistakes or failings.

'He kept screaming that I was selfish, calculating and lots of far nastier words,' said Karen, thirty-six, 'like he could order me to love him.' When someone is behaving so badly, it is easy to cast yourself as the innocent victim. However, in counselling, Karen began to look at the bigger picture. 'I put up with too much; I could have left earlier, but he would wheedle me round with promises and flowers and I would reward his manipulative behaviour by staying – even though my guts told me I wasn't right for him and he certainly wasn't right for me.' With a better understanding, Karen not only confirmed that she was right to leave but also learned a lesson that would stop her making the same mistake again.

In other cases, Leavers are so keen to find bland reasons for the break-up – such as 'circumstances' or 'we grew apart' or 'incompatibility' – that it is hard to take away anything to do differently next time round. It takes two people to make a relationship and two people to break it. A balanced understanding of why your relationship collapsed is empowering. It provides a strategy for personal change (rather than waiting for your partner to mend his or her ways) and either the possibility of saving the relationship or the chance to move on and make a better relationship next time round.

## What will be the impact on other people?

If the person most affected is your partner, it is much easier to leave. Pity is not a good enough foundation for a relationship. However, if you have a history of blowing hot when you are pursuing a new lover and cold when you have won them over, it would be wise to take a long look at your dating patterns. First, it would be unfair to make the same mistakes with someone else and second, you will benefit from understanding why you get cold feet. (There is more help on commit-ment issues in another book in this series: *Are You Right For Me?*) If the people who will be most affected are your friends or family – who feel this partner is just right for you – they will get over their disappointment (but you would benefit from understanding why their opinions count so much). However, if you have children with your partner, it is important to stop and think hard. If they knew that you were about to separate, what would they say? How would they feel? What would they ask you to do?

## Coping Day to Day

Looking into the future is frightening and this is particularly the case for the partner who would much rather save the relationship. When the University of Colorado studied 144 couples who had recently separated, they found that the partner who did not initiate the split was more likely to suffer, feel out of control and be distressed. It didn't seem to matter how unhappy the relationship had been. The anxiety increases significantly when separation turns from an idea into a reality.

Gary, a primary school teacher, found himself cut adrift from his normal routine when his partner of five years, Nicola, moved out and went to stay with her mother: 'I worried she would turn Nicola against me. I worried what friends would think. I worried whether I'd be able to afford the flat on my own. I worried that I would never taste her baked polenta with goat's cheese salad again.' To make matters worse Gary's brain was simultaneously churning over past memories of golden moments together, the pain of getting through that day and the void where the future used to be. At work, Gary was good at coping with emergencies but this time he felt completely de-skilled. In fact, he was facing the two biggest challenges for someone living through a temporary or trial separation: worry and over-analysing. Although they normally come as a pair, and feed off each other, they are subtly different. While worry is about what will happen in the future, over-analysing is normally about what happened in the immediate past. So what can be done to stop these twin enemies from overwhelming you?

## Paralysed by Worry

Cut through indecision and anxiety by adopting these strategies:

**Phase one:** Cut the future down into manageable chunks. Instead of stewing, often needlessly, about a distant tomorrow, try concentrating on getting through the next few weeks.

Instead of seeing Gary immobilised by the prospect of spending months and months of empty weekends without Nicola, I asked him to focus on that coming weekend. Which would be the dangerous moments? He had football on Saturday morning, so no problems there. What about Saturday night? He decided to arrange a drink with an old school friend. Sunday lunch was another problem so he would invite himself round to his parents. On Sunday evening he would be preparing for his next week at work, so he was happy to be home alone.

Once he had broken the weekend down, everything seemed more manageable, until he let his focus drift again. 'What about our summer holidays?' he asked, groaning. Normally I would sympathise, but in a crisis it is vital to concentrate on today. 'That's not your responsibility at the moment,' I told him. 'Your job is to make it through the next week.'

**Phase two:** Get the facts, as this will prevent worrying in a vacuum. Visit the Citizens' Advice Bureau or a solicitor – most are happy to give an initial consultation at a reduced fee – to find out where you stand financially and legally.

Next find a friend who will provide a sounding board and help you sort reasonable from unreasonable fears. Ideally, this friend should be someone who will just listen and not offer to wade into the crisis – as this will only complicate matters.

**Phase three:** Accept that everybody worries. It is a sensible and natural response. The goal should be to worry less about matters beyond your control – 'Will he phone?' or 'Will she want to see me this weekend?' – and concentrate more on things that you can change directly, such as your own behaviour.

During Gary and Nicola's trial separation, Nicola threw a Sunday afternoon barbecue to celebrate her birthday. She invited Gary, her parents, and various shared friends. Unfortunately, there was a disagreement between Nicola and her father, who insisted on grilling the meat his way. 'Nicola lost her temper and stormed back into the house. My instinct was to ignore the incident – even though they were really shouting,' Gary explained, 'but then I thought that's what I'd always done and what I'd always done had brought me to the point where I almost had to beg for an invite to her birthday party! I needed to change, but how?' He decided to do the opposite from normal and followed her inside. 'I listened to all her complaints about her dad, and she had a little weep. I kept thinking: what would I have done before? Probably offer to have a word with him. So, again, I told myself: Try something different. I just heard her out and, do you know, that seemed to be enough.'

The birthday party became a turning point for Gary and Nicola. While Gary's trick of finding a different approach from the past did not always come up trumps, it worked often enough to get them out of their relationship rut. Perhaps more importantly, he stopped worrying what Nicola would do next and focused instead on how he could be different.

## STOP WORRYING

The secret is to live in watertight compartments and not to stew needlessly about a distant tomorrow.

- Make a list of all your worries, and then cross off those that are not immediately relevant for the next month. If you are feeling very positive, try and bring your window of worry down to just the next week.
- With the remaining worries, write down three practical things to solve them.
- If you can't think of anything, make a deal with yourself and refuse to think about the worry for half an hour. Get some fresh air, as a walk can lift your spirits and help you to think things through.
- Ask yourself: What is the worst that could happen? Prepare yourself mentally to accept

the likely worst case and then expend your energy on calmly improving on it.

- Avoid caffeine and sugar and cut back on smoking and alcohol. All these are stimulants and will make your mind race even more.

- At night, if you can't sleep, picture your worries on the piece of paper. Tell yourself: 'There's nothing I can do now' and then imagine screwing up the paper and throwing it out of a pretend hole in your head. Do it several times until you are calmer.

## Over-analysing

While it is hard to find any benefits in worrying, the ability to really analyse a problem is normally an asset. However, the stress of an unwanted separation, or the threat of one, can tip useful introspection over into negative thoughts and, instead of fresh insights, offer only a distorted lens on the world. The person trying to save the relationship starts playing relationship detective: endlessly going over a telephone conversation for clues; dissecting how well a meeting with their beloved went; putting all the facts together to try and build a bigger picture. Over-analysing teases a million angles out of an issue until someone can no longer think straight and either becomes chronically indecisive or panicked into bad choices.

So how can you tell where healthy introspection ends and over-analysing begins? Normally the first will range over the whole of the relationship while the second focuses on events over the past few months – often to the exclusion of everything else. While healthy introspection will throw up new strategies for healing a relationship, over-analysing will send you round in circles and, ultimately, nowhere.

For example, Zoë did a lot of hard thinking after Murray told her that he didn't love her any more and many of her conclusions helped improve the relationship. However, after Murray asked for some space to get his head straight, Zoë went into overdrive. 'Everything became a clue to whether he was going to come back to me or not. How long did it take to return my text? Did he want to come round for Sunday lunch? Reports from a mutual friend over his state of mind seemed to take on a huge importance. If he seemed to be missing me, I'd be up in the clouds. If he was tired and wanted to go home early, I'd be depressed for days.' When Murray called during her down days, she'd be snappy and often on the attack, despite being pleased to hear from him. In our counselling sessions, Zoë learned to stop looking for a deeper meaning behind Murray's behaviour, to relax and enjoy her time with him. So what is the secret?

**Phase one:** Accept that over-analysing is not constructive. People keep doing it because they feel they are getting great insights and stripping away the rose-coloured glasses. However, more often than not someone who over-analyses ends up feeling bad about themselves or their partner. The next time you catch yourself over-analysing, put up a mental stop sign and distract yourself with something pleasant – like exercise or a hobby; play with the children or pick up a magazine. Eight minutes of distraction has been found to be enough to lift your mood and avoid depressing thoughts.

**Phase two:** Reschedule your thoughts. Tell yourself that you are not avoiding the problems but putting them off to a better time. When the rescheduled time comes, you may find that everything feels less overwhelming or that the problems have simply disappeared. This rescheduling is especially important in the evening, as it is best to avoid distressing thoughts before going to sleep.

**Phase three:** Commit your thoughts to paper. Do not censor yourself – rather like taking dictation – write down everything. Then look back over it and underline just the concrete events – not your interpretations. Keep on going back to these facts. Discuss them with a practical friend, who will look for solutions rather than be sympathetic, thus fanning the flames of over-analysing.

**Phase four:** Look for simplicity. In the majority of cases, the most straightforward interpretation of events is always the best. For example, probably Murray didn't return Zoë's text because he was in a meeting, not for any sinister reason.

In my experience, people who over-analyse fall into three main patterns: the *angry*, who end up blaming other people (like Zoë); the *self-critical*, who blame themselves; and the *swamped*, who become overwhelmed and are prone to becoming depressed. Which one do you fall into? Try the quiz on the next page.

# ARE YOU PRONE TO OVER-ANALYSING?

Although this quiz is a bit of fun, there is a serious side to it too. It will help you discover your analysing style and offer some specially targeted advice.

1. You have a blazing row with your partner and you find yourself repeating all those insults you promised you'd never use. Do you think:
   a) This is just one of many ways that I've let my partner down;
   b) I should make a grovelling apology – even if, deep down, you feel you were in the right;
   c) It's my partner's fault for provoking me;
   d) Arguments happen in even the best-regulated families?

2. You make an extra special effort to seduce your partner in the bedroom, but he or she rolls over and starts snoring. Do you think:
   a) If they are not interested in me, they must be getting it somewhere else. I knew that new member of their department was trouble;
   b) Considering how much weight I've put on, it's a miracle anyone ever fancies me;

c) My partner didn't thank me for preparing supper either; they always take me for granted, why did I ever fall for such a selfish man/woman?

d) My partner has probably been working too hard?

3. During a telephone conversation with your partner, there are a lot of awkward silences. Afterwards you find yourself dwelling on it. Do you think:

a) Why can't the two of us get on, and why do I keep rubbing everybody up the wrong way? Do I actually get on with anybody?

b) Maybe if I could be more tolerant, we could still be friends;

c) Why do I have to do all the work?

d) I'm not going to let it spoil my day?

4. During a temporary separation between you and your partner, one of your best friends has a dinner party to celebrate their birthday but invites neither you nor your partner. What is your reaction?

a) Could everybody have been talking about me behind my back and decided to deliberately exclude me?

b) Phone the member of the group that you're closest to and find out if you've done anything to upset the hostess;

c) I wouldn't have wanted to go anyway;

d) My friend probably couldn't fit everybody round the table, or maybe it would have been embarrassing to invite just me?

**5.** Your partner tells you that his or her mother was remarkably quiet when told the news about your problems. Trying to keep things light, you joke: 'Are you sure she hadn't been swapped with someone else's mother?' Your partner laughs. But later do you think:

a) He/she will be upset that I've run down his/her mother and think I'm not supportive enough. Worse still, I don't understand him/her and will never be told anything again;

b) I'm always putting my foot in it and must engage brain before mouth;

c) She deserved everything and more – the way she criticises everybody she had it coming to her;

d) If my partner is upset about my comments, he/she will say something about it?

**6.** Which is closest to your personal motto:
   a) There are more questions than answers;
   b) Must try harder;
   c) Why is everybody always picking on me?
   d) What you don't know can't harm you?

**7.** Your partner leaves a note asking to meet up that evening. Do you think:
   a) How will I tell the family we're splitting up and how will I ever find anybody who fancies me again?
   b) Go over every recent conversation again in your mind and work out what you have done to upset your partner;
   c) It's all his/her fault. How can he/she expect loyalty when they treat me like this?
   d) I'll find out what it's about soon enough?

**Mostly a): Swamped analysis**
In your head, your thoughts have logical connections – even if, in reality, they have nothing to do with each other. The result is that you are flooded and do not know where to turn.

**Breakthrough tip:** Next time you feel overwhelmed, stop and unpack all the different thoughts. Behind nearly every one will be someone else's voice telling you what to do – 'You should make the most of yourself'; 'You shouldn't let someone down'; 'You should always be nice' – until you are overwhelmed with a tyranny of 'should's. With each 'should' stop and ask yourself: Who says? Is their advice still appropriate today or in this situation?

**Mostly b): Self-critical analysis**

It is easy for you to talk yourself down and, despite being perfectly capable, you have a low opinion of yourself. Even when there is a positive spin on something, you will always take the opposite approach.

**Breakthrough tip:** First, you cannot change the past, so there is no point running yourself down. Second, learn to forgive yourself. With forgiveness, you do not get bogged down with guilt and can move on to solving the problem. Finally, when thinking back over something, ask yourself if you are giving too much weight to negative thoughts. Be aware that there are positive and neutral possibilities too.

**Mostly c): Angry analysis**

Although not quick to lose your temper, you often stew over things and end up feeling bitter.

Sometimes this can be a cold anger – often very deadly – on other occasions you simply explode. Because you do not like yourself in this mood, you try to avoid the problem with a quick-fix solution, which often leads to long-term complications and is fertile ground for future dissatisfaction.

**Breakthrough tip:** You have high expectations of yourself and everybody around you. However, life would be easier if you could sometimes accept things the way they are and move on. For example, when your practical mother is not more openly loving, embrace her good qualities rather than get angry about the rest. Next time somebody upsets you, do not think: 'How could they do this to me?' Instead learn to forgive and focus only on the real slights and what to do about them.

### Mostly d): Well-balanced analysis

You do not spend hours thinking something over unless it is a genuine crisis. When you make a decision, you stick to it. These are qualities to applaud. But are you sometimes too busy 'doing' to consider how other people might be feeling?

**Breakthrough tip:** In times of trouble, your level head is an asset. However, next time you find yourself playing back a difficult conversation, look for what is happening under the surface. What might have been left unspoken? By becoming aware of these extra dimensions you will probably make even better choices.

## Feeling Guilty

While worry and over-analysing is often a problem for Stickers, Leavers are more likely to be paralysed by guilt at this point in the journey. It is a perfectly natural human emotion and generally a very useful one. We feel guilty when we have done something that violates our personal value system and, assuming that we buy into them, society's values too. Guilt, therefore, has its positive side: not only does it bind people together but it also means that most citizens self-police and the courts intervene only in exceptional circumstances. However, when guilt turns toxic, there is normally another closely related emotion mixed in: shame. While guilt is about an action, for example: parking on double yellow lines, shame is about one's personal unworthiness. In other words, we feel we are a bad person rather than a good person doing something bad.

'If only I didn't feel so guilty,' said Ben, forty-one. He had been with his wife since they were both teenagers but he had fallen out of love. They were having a temporary separation so he could work out how he really felt. From his point of view, the separation had been going really well. 'I've had a chance to breathe, be myself and not just a husband and father.' However, family time was proving to be extremely painful. 'We went down to the seaside and the children had a wonderful time, catching things in rock pools and throwing sticks for the dog. Fiona and I got on really well, too, and for a while I think we all forgot that I lived in a flat round the corner. But after tea, I got up to go and the look on Fiona's face . . .' I know she wanted me to spend the night.' He buried his face in his hands. 'I know I'm being selfish but, if it's any consolation, I feel really guilty about it.' His guilt was paralysing him, stopping him from either moving forwards or backwards and, worse still, he was giving Fiona and his children very mixed signals.

Feelings of guilt can often be traced right back to childhood: 'If you're a good boy and finish that, you can have dessert' or 'Good girls go to the party; bad girls stay at home.' Some parents unconsciously add an extra message: 'If you don't behave, I will take my love away too.' This idea that 'good things happen to good people and bad things happen to bad people' is further reinforced by religion, schools and popular TV dramas – where virtuous characters are rewarded and the immoral suffer. With this in mind, it is no surprise that everybody likes to view themselves in the best possible light.

Indeed, Ben admitted: 'I can't be a bad person because a bad person wouldn't feel so guilty about needing space.' In effect, the guilt was allowing Ben to still view himself as a good man. Guilt also protected him from looking at other difficult feelings: anger; pain; grief; regrets; if only I'd done this; if only I hadn't done that. Instead of engaging with these monsters, Ben would try to tame his guilt by phoning his kids or distract himself by going for a beer with his work colleague. These coping mechanisms were fine, up to a point, but did nothing to address the underlying causes. While most emotions burn themselves out, toxic guilt can last for ever. Ben might have hated the guilt but he felt even more uncomfortable about the feelings hidden behind it.

So instead of suppressing or ignoring your guilty feelings, try analysing them. On the one hand, the guilt could mean that you are doing something that violates your personal code and your conscience is telling you to stop; or, on the other hand, you could be taking more than your share of the responsibility for the relationship crisis.

## THE GUILT JOURNAL

Buy a ring-bound exercise book, rather than using odd pieces of paper, as you will need to refer back. This exercise also involves a lot of writing and buying a nice notebook will show a commitment to persevere.

1. **Confess.** Instead of the thoughts going round in your head, write down everything in your guilt journal. Some of the guilty feelings will be about past events and some of them will be fresh today; it doesn't matter if the two types of guilt are mixed up. However, put the date at the top of each entry, so that you can look back and discover which guilty thought preoccupied you and when. Don't worry about style, spelling or grammar – just let everything go in a stream of consciousness.

2.  **Analyse.** You will be more objective if there is a gap of two or three days between writing and analysing. Take a marker pen and go back over what you have written and start looking for black-and-white thinking. Words like 'always' and 'never' are good clues. Next try and find thoughts that suggest superhero skills and second sight, and mark these up too. Sentences with words like 'should' or 'ought' are often indicators of this kind of thinking. Finally, look for sentences that impart blame and underline them too. Maybe one colour for yourself and one for your partner. How do the different colours balance up?

3.  **Identify the main themes.** Although guilt can throw up a thousand and one variations, there is normally only a handful of main themes. Give your theme, or each of your themes, a name. For example: guilt about not supporting your partner enough while their father was dying could be *hospice*.

4.  **Questionnaire.** For each theme, jot down some thoughts under the following headings:
    • What could you have done differently?
    • Thinking of that time, what resources would you have needed?

- What prevented you from doing it?
- What do you feel angry about?
- Who are you angry with?
- What could you learn for the future?

5. **Reflect.** Put away your journal for a week and return to it later with fresh eyes. Read through everything and allow yourself to grieve for past mistakes before taking stock about what comes next.

6. **Reopen the journal and answer just one more question:** How can I make amends? Write down as many practical solutions as possible, even if some of them seem ridiculous at the time. After you have exhausted all the possibilities – both sane and insane – go back and select the most appropriate.

## The Bigger Picture

One of the most useful adjustments is to pull the focus wider than just your relationship and think about other factors that might be behind the unhappiness. American marketing guru Abraham Maslow sets out a hierarchy of needs which shows that when basic requirements have been satisfied, we move on to higher aspirations. For example, once someone has a full belly, he or she can worry about somewhere safe to live and then about a relationship and being loved. In the fifties, when Maslow set out his theory, he felt the average consumer was satisfied 80 per cent of the time in their physiological needs, 70 per cent in their safety needs, 50 per cent of the time in belonging and love needs, and 40 per cent in self-esteem/ prestige/status, but only satisfied for 10 per cent of the time for the top need, which he called self-actualisation: personal fulfilment and self-realisation of potential.

Looking at commercials today, products such as soft drinks are no longer aimed at quenching our thirst, a basic physiological need, but offering the illusion of satisfying our higher needs – such as identity. Marriage seems to have been climbing the same ladder. Our grandparents placed more emphasis on being a good provider/housekeeper. Twenty-five years ago, when I first saw couples professionally, they were asking for more love and companionship. Today people are asking their partners for the highest need of all: 'Help me become the best that I can be.' Although many social commentators complain that we expect too much from relationships, I think this only becomes a problem when it collides with another twenty-first-century phenomenon: denying ageing.

The average age at divorce in Britain, according to the Office for National Statistics, is now 42.3 for men and 39.8 for women. Turning forty, and the mid-life crisis, is normally treated as the butt of a joke: 'What's the best way to cover a bald spot?' Answer: a Porsche. We are encouraged, in particular, to laugh at men sucking in their paunches and reliving their glory days by buying fast bikes and cars, or dating much younger women. For some reason society has no equivalent stereotype for women, yet I counsel many who are dealing with similar mid-life problems.

However, I do not use the term 'mid-life crisis' in my counselling, as men are quick to disassociate themselves from the idea – although their wives might think it appropriate. Often when, as part of my standard assessment, I ask both male and female clients when their problems started, they will immediately protest: 'It has nothing to do with turning forty.' The second reason I avoid the term is because the problems can strike at any time. In fact, books have been written about the quarter-life crisis: twenty-five-year-olds who feel time is running out. My final objection to 'mid-life crisis' is that it does not have to be a crisis with all the drama that implies.

The death of a loved one, often a parent, can also be a wake-up call. There is no more concrete proof that we are not immortal than sitting at your mother or father's hospital or hospice bedside, and witnessing their decline. Even more startling is the death of a contemporary – perhaps in a car accident or, worse still, some illness – as the illusion that mortality belongs to the generation above is stripped away. Finally, everybody faces the truth that their time on earth is finite. At this point some people will ask: 'What is the meaning of life?', or 'How can I make sense of my own life?' Others will decide that life is too short to be unhappy or in an unhappy relationship and search for remedies.

It is during this existential questioning that many people reach for self-actualisation: the highest level of Maslow's hierarchy of needs. According to Maslow: 'Discontent and restlessness will soon develop, unless the individual is doing what he is fitted for. A musician must make music, an artist must paint and a poet must write if he is to be ultimately at peace with himself. What a man can be, he must be.' At first sight this seems a perfectly feasible goal; except most professions today are not as clear-cut as musician, artist or poet.

What about the people whose work is made up of hundreds of different tasks with no clear-cut core? What about the others who don't particularly like their work and have no desire to be the best-ever accounts clerk? Maslow tried to study what self-actualisation might be like, but found it extremely difficult to find people who met his criteria. In the end, he had to settle for just forty-five people: a strange combination of personal friends and acquaintances; twenty students who seemed to be developing in the direction of self-actualisation; plus historical and contemporary figures.

Unfortunately, becoming everything that one is capable of becoming seems to run the risk of destroying other people en route. Even a cursory reading of the biographies of the famous suggests that although we might enjoy their music, books, films, etc., we would probably not wish to be married to them. Even Maslow warns that the road to self-actualisation could be a blind alley: 'Higher needs are less perceptible, less unmistakable, more easily confused with other needs by suggestion, imitation, by mistaken belief or habit.' We must remember that Maslow comes from an era before advertising, marketing and public relations became as sophisticated and all-pervasive as they are today. Nowadays we have to be very watchful otherwise, instead of truly discovering ourselves, we are sold a holiday on a Greek island, a bottle of beer or a new car.

## A Spiritual Crisis?

Ultimately, underneath the so-called mid-life crisis and striving for self-actualisation, there is probably a search for spirituality: making sense of the world beyond the self-centred and materialistic. For some people this can also include a search for some greater power, either mystical or religious. Certainly, when listening to Leavers talk about their future life – the expected bliss, fulfilment, contentment and even completeness – I am often reminded of a spiritual quest.

A good example would be Martin, a thirty-eight-year-old salesman: 'Some mornings while I stand on the platform waiting for the 7.50, I start thinking, "What's it all about?" Surely, there is something more than daily reports and targets. I want my time to count – rather than just filling the hours until the next day when I will be standing in the same place again watching the same discarded newspaper supplements blow across the rails. If I started again, there would not only be space and time to think but also the possibility of meeting someone who would make even the seconds count.' For Martin love had become the passport out of his mundane existence into a better tomorrow. Although 'limerence' might, temporarily, have the power to transform, it cannot last for ever and while loving someone makes for a more complete life, on its own it cannot make an empty life meaningful.

So if not with love alone, how can we make life more purposeful? Why are we here? What is the meaning of life? How do I fill this void at the centre of my life? These are profound questions; unfortunately, all the books and potential answers are either full of platitudes or leave one thinking: yes, but so what? I believe the problem is that each of us has to find our own answer: something that fits our world-view, the issues from our particular upbringing and, ultimately, confronts our unique doubts, questions and personality. My answer is not going to be your answer, but at the risk of adding to the pile of platitudes, I will share my thoughts about creating a fulfilled life in the hope that they might kick-start yours:

## Create rather than just consume

Instead of watching sport on TV, go out and play one. Instead of grabbing a convenience meal, take the time to cook something from scratch. Alternatively, take an adult education class in pottery, music, creative writing; the list is endless. Sadly, we live in an age that only values something if it earns money, but don't let this common misconception stop you. If a hobby brings you pleasure, do it.

## The journey is more important than the destination

Travelling with an open mind and heart is more important than where one ultimately arrives. With this attitude, how quickly your contemporaries' travel becomes less important and the risk of pointless jealousy subsides. If life is a race, something I doubt, at least think of it as a marathon rather than a sprint.

## Embrace death as a constant travelling companion

After suffering a major bereavement in my thirties, I learned that death could be a friend rather than the enemy. With every major decision, or fork on the journey, I am always aware of the time limit on life, and love, and am guided to make the fullest use of my share of it. Richard Holloway, formerly Bishop of Edinburgh, puts this more poetically in his book *Looking in the Distance: The Human Search For Meaning.* He concludes with: 'Our brief finitude is but a beautiful spark in the vast darkness of space. So we should live the fleeting day with passion and, when the night comes, depart from it with grace.'

## Final Adjustments

This step gives both Leavers and Stickers a greater understanding of the past and a more realistic idea of the future. However, it is easy to lose sight of the skills needed for negotiating a way through day-to-day life. So at this point in the journey, I ask my clients to put every dilemma to this test:

*What's in my power?*

Donald and Deborah were making great progress. He had begun to stand in his wife's shoes: 'She does have a case, I haven't been a particularly good husband. Although I'd still like the chance to change that, she seems to have moved on.' He had also decided to forge a better relationship with his children. Meanwhile, Deborah had understood that Donald needed more time to come to terms with the end of their relationship. Although she stopped coming to counselling, she agreed not to tell the children just yet and for them all to continue to live together for the time being. However, the next week, Donald arrived for his solo session looking depressed and despondent. 'I really lost it with Deborah. I try to shoulder my share of looking after the kids but she won't let me. For example, she was late back and instead of phoning and telling me so that I could start food, she rushed in at the last moment and threw something out of the microwave on to the table.' He felt helpless and the situation seemed hopeless.

So I asked to him to focus on: *What's in my power?* 'I can't change Deborah's mind and going off on one of my rants just makes matters worse,' he said. 'However, I could have cooked for the children. If I'm making something from scratch, I really enjoy it.' The next week, he came back smiling. 'I did a cooked breakfast on Sunday for the children and they really enjoyed it. Deborah was a bit sniffy. She thinks I'm making "too much fuss" but I felt I'd made a step forward.' Instead of focusing on what he couldn't change, he had remembered: *What's in my power?*

## Summing Up

When a relationship is breaking down, the Leaver can often have unrealistic ideas about how much splitting up will solve. Conversely, the Sticker will have too rosy a picture of the relationship and of how easy it will be to resolve ingrained problems. During the adjustment step, both partners step back and get a clearer picture. Although this process is both tough and very sobering, it is the beginning of the healing.

### NUTSHELLS FOR LEAVERS:

- It takes real courage to face up to long-term problems and to call an end to the suffering.
- Although it is kinder to soft-pedal the reasons for the breakdown with your partner – unless they ask for a full post-mortem – be honest with yourself and learn the lessons for the future.
- Instead of trying to change your partner's reaction to the split, concentrate on what's within your power: your own behaviour.

**NUTSHELLS FOR STICKERS:**

- Instead of putting all your effort into trying to save the relationship, step back and learn about yourself and what you need.
- Focus on immediate issues over the next seven days, rather than worrying about the future or obsessing about the past.
- Look at your own behaviour. Does it make communication easier or does it reinforce the barriers between you and your partner?

STEP 4

# ACCEPTANCE

As the reality of breaking up begins to sink in, and the loss really hits home, many people try to distract themselves: some will have a makeover or take out a gym membership, others will bury themselves in work. In the first difficult weeks there is no right or wrong approach – what's important is for people to find something to help them make it through. However, after this first flush of energy, most recently separated people discover that they need to understand the past before moving forward. Slowly but surely, often over a bottle of wine, they will rake over what happened with their friends or family. It might be painful, but ultimately it is the right thing to do.

In a paper presented to the British Psychological Society Conference, Dr Carla Willig of London's City University identified three main stories ex-lovers commonly use to describe what went wrong: 'There's such a strong need to have an explanation,' she claims, 'and those people who haven't got one find the break-up more difficult to accept. Of the people I studied, there was just one man with no story. He was still struggling through his pain many years later.'

## Telling the Story of Your Break-up

Michelle is a twenty-seven-year-old TV researcher, whose husband Claude disappeared for two months and reappeared on the other side of the world. Nearly two years later, she was still having trouble making sense of her divorce: 'I don't have any answers, that's what makes it so hard. We only spoke a couple of times on the phone, but that's it. I just don't have a proper explanation. What possessed him to just disappear?'

It is tempting to think that an ex holds the answer – and that is certainly the motivation behind a lot of late-night, slightly drunken calls – but, ultimately, these conversations never get anywhere. Each half of a separating couple has to build up his or her own account of what happened and why. In fact, on many occasions, these stories will be radically different. Slowly I helped Michelle piece together what had happened. Her husband Claude did not like conflict and never argued. 'He just seemed happy to go along with what I suggested,' she explained. What if Claude did not agree? 'He'd just keep it to himself. I suppose the pressure of bottling it up was just too much,' she answered. It seemed that Claude had taken avoiding conflict to its ultimate extreme and just disappeared. Michelle had begun to put her story together.

Another example is Kelvin, who wrote to my website: 'I am forty-eight and six months ago broke up with my boyfriend who is thirty-six. One Sunday, after three years' committed relationship (but not living together), my partner suddenly walked out (after we had spent a great Saturday together). He became very emotional and simply asked me to let him go, but would not explain what was wrong or his reasons for leaving. I had no choice but to let him go. The next four months were very difficult as he would not return my calls. Before he walked out I had no idea there was a problem and he has since acknowledged that he gave me no signs he was about to leave. However, we met up and he was emotionally drawn to me once more. This pattern of walking out, but not explaining why, happened for a second time twelve months later. After we had split up, he did eventually agree to counselling. After four sessions, with little understanding about the relationship dynamics, I was surprised that he wanted to give our relationship a third chance – but to review things after six months. However, two months after getting back together the shutters came down and he left for the final time.' Kelvin's distress was multiplied not just by being let down so often but by having no explanation.

So what types of stories to describe what went wrong has Dr Willig found? The first story – *To The Bitter End* – is built around the idea of doomed lovers. From the first kiss, every twist in the tale is painful. Every jealous event, bad holiday and discovered secret is used to illustrate how the relationship had problems all along. The reality of the relationship might, in fact, have been very different. But these former lovers use a cut-and-burn technique to obliterate all the tender memories and then to move on. Sadly, I meet some people who think the whole relationship has been invalidated by the split. Roberta had been married for fifteen years and had a twelve-year-old daughter, but when her husband threatened divorce, she said: 'I'm so angry with him. I feel that he has stolen my best years and I can never get them back. Everything is ruined.' With this mindset, even the good times at the beginning of the relationship hold the seeds for the ending and are somehow tainted. It is like looking back at a holiday while stranded at the airport waiting for the flight home and feeling the whole trip was a disaster. However, no matter how much discomfort there is during the hold-up, it cannot undo the pleasure experienced at the beginning of the holiday of eating calamari while overlooking the old fishing port.

The second story – *A Way Out* – builds on a similar principle. From the beginning something has been not quite right: the lovers had incompatible habits or different interests. He might have been tidy, for example, while she left her knickers on the bathroom floor; or she might have been a computer expert while he was an artist. However, while the 'bitter enders' let these small painful events build until one final event breaks the camel's back, the 'way outers' find a dramatic exit. In Dr Willig's study this was nearly always an affair, with another lover providing an excuse for the ending.

The third story – *Changed Circumstances* – is an entirely different narrative. This relationship starts well. After a honeymoon period, the couple settle down into a happy life together. However, the course of true love does not run smooth and, as in all stories, there are obstacles to overcome. One partner is promoted and their job takes them away; the children leave home; or the couple simply grow apart – all these new circumstances can undermine what was once a happy relationship.

Dr Willig's research also explains why men are more likely than women to be emotionally damaged by relationship break-up. Previously experts simply blamed men's tendency to keep problems bottled up but it goes deeper than this. By not talking, men are failing to construct an ending for their relationship. By contrast, women, while off-loading on to friends, are forever rehearsing and finally settling on a version for their break-up. Whether these explanations are right or wrong is immaterial. 'Any account is better than none,' claims Dr Willig.

## An Alternative Story

However, Michelle's story does not entirely fit into any of the three stories identified by Dr Willig. This is why I add a fourth narrative. I call it the 'Unwanted Opportunity' and it works for both the Leaver and the Sticker. 'We had a good and fulfilling relationship which worked for a while,' this story says. 'We both made mistakes and ultimately we went in different directions. Being single is not what I wanted but I am determined to see the opportunities rather than dwelling on what I've lost.' 'Unwanted Opportunity' people use the painful experiences to hone their relationship skills. So when they meet someone in the future, they will make the most of it. Many people move on to this fourth narrative after having first used one of the other stories, so arriving here is proof that you have made progress.

## PUT YOUR BREAK-UP UNDER THE SPOTLIGHT

This simple test will help you decide which story to tell:

1. Which statement best describes your arguments?
   a) He/she never listened.
   b) We tried to resolve our problems but slipped back into old ways.
   c) We didn't argue very much.
   d) Somehow we could never get through to each other.

**2.** Which statement best describes your sex life?

   a) Fireworks more times than not.

   b) We got bored in bed.

   c) Satisfactory but not earth-moving.

   d) We had our good times and bad times.

**3.** Which statement best describes your break-up?

   a) I'm better off without them.

   b) The affair was a catalyst, not the cause.

   c) We became like brother and sister.

   d) Maybe we could become friends sometime in the future.

**4.** Which statement best describes how you're left feeling?

   a) I don't know how I put up with him/her for so long.

   b) It could have dragged on for much longer.

   c) It was just one of those things.

   d) As long as I learn something, that's the important thing.

**5.** Which statement best describes your feelings about meeting someone else?

   a) Forget it – not with my track record.

   b) I'm frightened to let anybody get close.

c) I'll have to wait and see.

d) I'm generally optimistic.

**Mostly a)**

You're a 'bitter ender'. At least the sex was probably good; many people put up with poor relationships because of the magic of making up after
a fight. However, try and see the relationship in
less black-and-white terms; life is normally drawn
from a far richer palette. The main advantage with
such a final ending: you are spared the charade of
pretending to stay friends.

**Mostly b)**

You are a 'way outer'. Beware of a tendency to
rewrite history to make your previous relationship
seem worse than it was and thereby reduce your
guilt. The aftermath of an affair often produces
increased levels of jealousy caused by a height-
ened awareness of how easily relationships break
up. There is also a possibility that you might want
to return to the original relationship after time and
distance has made you reassess what you've lost.

**Mostly c)**

You're a 'changed circumstancer'. Remember
that a relationship needs the right environment

to flourish; just loving each other is not always enough. These good relationships can also peter out because each person swallows their differences to preserve the happy picture and nothing gets solved. The positives are that you are unlikely to blame yourself or your lover, so there is always the possibility of salvaging a proper friendship.

**Mostly d)**

You are an 'unwanted opportunity', which suggests that you are making good progress. However, do not be surprised if there are times when you feel depressed or angry; recovery is never a straight line and most people will fall back from time to time. If you find yourself stuck in one of these holes, it may be worth considering counselling to find a fresh perspective.

## Dealing with Regrets

When looking back over a relationship, many people feel a complete failure and find only one person to blame: themselves. Weighed down by a million regrets, and a thousand things they should have done better, they become depressed and start despairing. However, I would recommend coming from a fresh angle. Machiavelli, the founder of political thinking, wrote a pamphlet entitled *The Prince*, in which he advised the ruling Medici family on how to keep power and influence events in their favour. He is famously ruthless but still wrote: 'I believe that it is probably true that fortune is the arbiter of half the things that we do, leaving the other half or so to be controlled by ourselves.' Yet most of us act as if the proportion we control is much larger and end up castigating ourselves.

Michelle, whose husband disappeared, took on all the blame: 'I keep thinking that I drove him away; I should have asked what he wanted,' she said. However, through counselling, she found a more balanced picture: 'He could have said something if he was unhappy. When I spoke to his mother, she told me that he had disappeared without explanation as a teenager, too.' Michelle had found a more fifty-fifty share for the break-up of her relationship.

If taking all the responsibility for a break-up is a mistake, so is going to the opposite extreme and blaming someone else. It might initially be comforting to feel 'it was not my fault' and that either circumstances or the other person's wicked-ness were to blame. However, in the long term, playing victim makes it harder to find someone new. Instead of saying: 'They took advantage of me', rephrase this as 'I should have stood up for myself more.' The first explanation leaves you vulnerable to repeat performances; the second explanation leads to an assertiveness course. In all good films and books, the hero or heroine learns something about themselves from their trials and tribulations. It is what makes satisfying drama; it also makes for a more satisfying life.

Although it is hurtful when one partner blames the other for the end of a relationship, or alternatively takes on all the blame, it should not be taken to heart. One of the few advantages of splitting up is that the ex's take on events no longer matters. Each half of the couple is heading for a different future and even if one ex-partner has a different story, it will not hamper the other's progress.

## TIME LINES

When constructing the story of how a relationship ended, some people become fixated on the last painful section and feel overwhelmed. To get a better perspective, take a piece of paper and create a graph: on the horizontal axis write 'time' and on the vertical axis mark 'pleasure' and 'pain' (see opposite). The first meeting with your partner is the zero point on the time axis; from there plot your whole relationship on to the graph with all the peaks and troughs. Label all the good times so that you do not forget them. Next, examine the bad times. Were they inevitable? What is the balance between positive and negative?

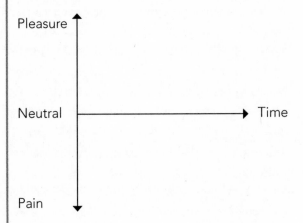

Roberta used this idea to look back over her fifteen-year marriage. She had a high for the birth of her daughter and after that everything was more or less a flat line. Beyond the last three and a half years, Roberta's graph showed that her relationship had been better than she had painted it. 'Obviously, I have regrets but actually it was not all bad,' she concluded.

# Five Stages of Grief

These were originally outlined by the Swiss-born psychiatrist Elisabeth Kübler-Ross, who wrote the seminal book *On Death and Dying* (Simon & Schuster, 1969). She had been working with terminally ill patients in New York and noticed that they moved through five stages: denial, anger, bargaining, depression and acceptance. Although Kübler-Ross's prime aim was to help doctors approach the dying with sensitivity and understanding, her stages have been transferred wholesale into bereavement counselling without taking into consideration that losing someone is a totally different experience from dying. With that note of caution, the five stages *are* useful for coming to terms with loss – whether through death, divorce or relationship breakdown – because they show that our feelings are natural, healthy and very human.

Here are her five stages:

## Denial

The first response to bad news is numbness: 'No, it can't be happening to me.' Denial is like a buffer against the shock. It provides us with a breathing space to collect our thoughts, find our coping strategies and gather our supporters. For Carrie, fifty-six, who ended her thirty-year marriage, it was like waking up from a long sleep: 'I remember looking round the family dinner table one Christmas and knowing that I could not do this for another year. Suddenly, I realised that I had been fooling myself. My husband would never change and the relief . . . it flooded through me. It was only then that I understood just how sad I had been.'

## Anger

The evidence is impossible to ignore. Finally, the truth dawns: 'Oh yes, it really is happening.' The next emotion is anger: 'Why me?' 'What have I done?' Generally, there are two kinds of anger. The first makes complete sense – after all, we are very hurt – and is normally aimed at our partners (for betraying our love and trust) and ourselves (either for our mistakes or for not spotting the seriousness earlier). I call this kind: rational anger. The second sort of anger, however, is completely different. Although we need to be angry, we dare not show it to our partners (especially if we are trying to persuade them to stay).

Instead, the feelings are dumped on to someone else. For example, the person who told us that our partner had been cheating, the other man or woman in the triangle, or our partner's family for 'encouraging' the break-up. I call this kind: irrational anger.

For the person who is left, the anger often lasts longer – especially if their partner has been unfaithful – and the ensuing depression phase involves a greater sense of being betrayed. Mark, twenty-eight, speaks for a lot of people: 'I would have done anything for Francesca but it was never enough. I just think of those hours retiling the bathroom, lining up the patterns, and all the thanks I got was when she described my work as "nice". I lost it, but she just stood there calmly, saying, "You can't guilt me into staying." When I think about her with anybody else, I have this knot inside my stomach and I fear it's never going to go away.' In some ways it is harder to grieve when you have been divorced, rather than bereaved, as the rejection is more personal and the ending less final. If you find yourself continually angry and unable to move on to the next stage, there is help in another book in this series: *Resolve Your Differences*.

## Bargaining

All the anger has changed nothing. So the coping strategies begin. As children, we learned that demanding something seldom brings what we want. So we tried asking nicely, being on our best behaviour or volunteering to do something round the house in return for having our wishes granted. In many ways, grief turns us into small children again: not in control of our destiny. So we regress and try to strike a bargain: 'Please stay for my fortieth birthday celebrations' or 'Let's make wild, passionate love and pretend everything is OK.' Bargaining is fine in the short term but all it does is postpone the inevitable.

## Depression

Still nothing has changed and we sink into depression. However, it is very important to stress that depression can be a healthy part of mourning. If we can allow depression to teach us – rather than blank it out with drink, chocolate and other coping strategies – it will become a vital part of our recovery.

There are two elements to depression. The first, Kübler-Ross called reactive: a natural response to loss. The second is preparatory and is linked with the part of depression where people retreat into themselves and want to do nothing but pull the duvet over their head or sit silently on the sofa. Shutting down and retreating from the clutter of everyday life allows us to concentrate our brain power into problem-solving. In effect, we need to imagine an end before we can cope with it and breaking down the problem is a necessary part of building something new. Like many people who wanted a divorce, Carrie was surprised by the depression that followed. 'My husband did everything to hold on to me. But, in the end, I just thought – you can have the house. I want to be free. So I thought I'd be celebrating my decree nisi, but when it arrived in the post I just sat at the bottom of the stairs and wept.' Although she had longed for the divorce, she still needed to mourn. 'There was a barrier between me and the rest of the world, but I suppose that it had to happen. I'd been really pumped up with adrenaline from all the fighting and when it was over I deflated quicker than a balloon.' Eventually, Carrie was able to look back at this period of depression as valuable. 'I suppose I needed to lick my wounds and it was probably better to stay at home and recover than to go out partying.'

## Acceptance

Once the anger and the depression have been worked through, we come to the reward. We might not want the relationship to end but we will finally accept the inevitable. Although there was hope in some of the previous stages, it has been a flickering candle and one easily blown out; during acceptance the flame shines brightly.

# What Stops People Reaching Acceptance?

By this stage in the healing process, it is good to pause and realise how far you have come. If you are the Leaver, you have broken through denial and realised the full extent of your relationship's problems. If you are the Sticker, you have survived being blasted straight into crisis by your partner's decision to leave. Acceptance of the break-up might not yet be a daily reality but it is no longer an impossible dream. 'It's still hard but I can see that things will improve,' said Donald, whom we have followed in earlier chapters. 'I accept that I'm going to be happier – even if that still seems a long way off.'

Neither my programme to *heal and move on* nor Kübler-Ross's five stages of grief is a simple ladder to be climbed rung by rung. Discovering new information – like your partner has found a new partner or told untruths about the split to your children – can send you back to crisis again. Don't despair. You will climb back up towards Acceptance and there is good news: the journey back is generally quicker the second, third and fourth time. However, sometimes the Leaver or the Sticker will adopt coping strategies which might assuage guilt or keep dim hopes of a reconciliation alive – and therefore ease pain in the short term – but which ultimately make it harder to reach Acceptance.

## Not wanting to hurt the other person

Breaking up is a messy business, and sadly it is impossible to do it painlessly. Sometimes the partner who wants to leave will hold back the news until after an important event – like a holiday together. However, once the other party finds out, this just increases the pain or provides another thing to be angry about.

Liza is a writer who had trouble recovering from an abusive boyfriend. She had tried to keep things civil between them, so she included his name on round robin emails which told friends and colleagues when her plays were being performed. Naturally, he turned up to watch them. When I questioned whether this was wise, since just being in the same room put her on edge, Liza replied: 'He won't think that he's a friend, because I kiss friends on the cheeks and I make a pointed decision not to kiss him.' I doubt whether he would have registered such a subtle rejection.

**Breakthrough tip:** Ultimately, it is always kinder to be direct when dealing with your ex. Otherwise throwaway comments to ease the pain – 'Who knows what the future may bring?' or 'Maybe one day' – can be misinterpreted as hopeful.

## Trying to be friends too soon

Nearly every couple that I counsel who decide to separate vow to stay friends. This is a laudable goal – especially if you have children – but a hard one to pull off. Mark and Francesca had been at university together and had a large circle of shared friends. 'It seemed natural to invite her to my birthday celebration at a local restaurant,' says Mark, 'except that I got upset because she wouldn't sit next to me. She sat as near the door as possible and left straight after the cake. It sort of ruined the evening.' Originally they had separated because of Francesca's affair and when that ended, Mark helped her move into a new flat – because that's what friends do. When Francesca had a problem with her boiler, he would drop everything and fix it. 'It took me a long time to realise that while Francesca was making a new life for herself, I was looking for signs that we could go back to the old one.'

**Breakthrough tip:** It's a big leap from lover to friend and it's impossible to make the transition overnight. So take a three-month break before meeting up again. If you have children, contact is inevitable but keep it down to factual exchanges about your kids.

## Fighting over 'a matter of principle'

This is normally a sign that one or both partners is trying to punish the other and is looking for the courts to prove their 'goodness' and their ex-partner's 'badness'. This is nearly always a dead-end and only increases the pain. It is far better to be rational, to try and solve old arguments and contain new ones. 'I really lost it when I discovered that my wife did not inform me about my son's school concert,' said Clive, thirty-six. 'She has deliberately tried to keep me out of his life. She can't accept that although I've left her, it doesn't mean that I want to leave my children.' 'But our son wasn't even in the concert; it was just a concert at his school, by some professional musicians, that he and I went to together,' said his wife, Natalie, thirty-eight. 'What do I have to do? Report all my movements?'

**Breakthrough tip:** Although bottling up our feelings can be destructive, unleashing them unedited on to our partner – what I call emoting – is equally problematic. Huge torrents of emotions not only pump up our hurt but also distort our feelings out of all recognition. So try the alternative and report your feelings. For example, Clive could have told Natalie: 'I felt hurt and excluded.' She could have told him: 'I felt hurt and misunderstood.' This reporting of their feelings (rather than emoting) would have eased communication and avoided a pointless fight.

## Obsessing

The relationship might be over but one partner is determined to stay in the life of the other – if only at a distance. This can include behaviour like phoning and hanging up, driving past their home or meeting up with mutual friends in order to elicit snippets of information. Danielle, twenty-nine, went even further: 'I would Google him to see if there was anything new; I knew his email password so I'd read his mail and I'd do other web-stalking-type stuff.' She had worked at the same company as her ex – albeit at different branches – and therefore shared a staff Christmas party. 'It was like a military operation. I spent weeks dieting, exercising and shopping for the "look what you're missing" dress. You should have seen his face. We ended up back at his place and it was incredible. Except that the next morning nothing had changed. I'd thought it was make-up sex but for him it was break-up sex.' Ultimately, obsessing takes up so much energy there is no room in your life for anything else.

**Breakthrough tip:** Next time you feel the need to 'check up' on your ex or indulge in other obsessive behaviour, stop and ask yourself: What is the feeling that I am trying to prevent? Is it anger or depression? What is my fear? Remember, these distractions are holding you back from healing and the opportunity to reach acceptance.

## Revenge

Typical strategies include sleeping with your ex's best friend, spreading nasty rumours, smashing up prized property and refusing access to the children or a shared pet. 'I thought if only I could hurt Callum as much as he hurt me, I'd feel better,' explained Kate, twenty-nine, in her counselling session. She had found that he was selling his house and posed as a possible buyer. 'I was deliberately only available when he was at work so that I would be taken round by the estate agent. When she was on her phone, I tore up a couple of pictures, rearranged the fridge magnets into a swear word and poured mouthwash on to his mattress – so it would look like he'd peed in his bed. I went home cackling – even though he would have guessed that it was me.' Although Kate claimed the revenge made her feel good, with a little probing she soon admitted that it made her also hate herself.

**Breakthrough tip:** Revenge not only encourages the other party to reciprocate – which further pumps up our anger – but it also binds us to our ex for even longer. So next time you're tempted, try the opposite and do something nice – like returning some treasured possession. In the long term, it will make you feel better.

## Hopeless devotion

Even though the relationship is dead – or totally without any viable future – one half of the couple is still holding on with both hands. These people get a perverse pleasure from the tragic elements of lost love; for example, rereading old love letters, playing torch songs that remind them of their beloved or watching weepie black-and-white movies. 'Our love was pure, a shining beacon in the mediocrity of everyday life,' explained Cassandra, fifty-two. 'Halfway through our first weekend together, we were sitting at a pavement café – it was the first sunny day of spring – and he said, "I can't imagine not being with you." I knew I'd never heard truer words and we toasted them with champagne.' However, six months later, her lover's firm posted him back to Egypt. Cassandra wanted to follow him but discovered he had a wife and children.

It was a tough blow and her friends were initially supportive but, six years later, have lost patience. Especially if the relationship was reasonably short-lived, it is better to learn from it and move on.

**Breakthrough tip:** In therapy, I often find people with hopeless devotions are more attached to the fantasy of perfect love than the real flesh-and-blood person. So how do you move on? Make a deal with yourself not to feed the fantasy. Stop listening to 'special songs' and put treasured items in a drawer or into the loft. If you start daydreaming about 'if only' scenarios, divert yourself by doing something vigorous like scrubbing the kitchen floor or occupy your brain with a crossword puzzle.

## Negative thinking

When someone is tired, stressed or reminded just how much he or she is about to lose, it is easy to put the worst possible spin on things. Sometimes people will even congratulate themselves for their 'honesty' with themselves. Occasionally, there can be a desire to punish the other partner: 'Look what you've done to me.'

However, the ability to find the positives will hasten your arrival to Acceptance. For example,

Donald found that he enjoyed evenings when Deborah was out: 'I can have a relationship with the children without feeling that Deborah is looking over my shoulder and disapproving. The other positive is that I've finally done something for myself – taking up golf – and I've realised Deborah was right. There was only work, duty and obligation in our lives. We need some joy, too.' When he found himself slipping back into negative thinking ('We're going to have to tell the children and then she'll move into the spare room'), I asked him for the positive ('It will be easier to sleep alone rather than with the Great Wall of China down the middle of the bed and a daily reminder that she doesn't want me').

**Breakthrough tip:** Sometimes the best way to rediscover a positive mood is to laugh. Often the funniest moments come out of the bleakest circumstances, so don't be afraid to step back and find the absurdity in your situation.

## HOW TO SWITCH OFF THOSE LOVING FEELINGS

Love can be an addiction, a physical craving that only the beloved can fulfil. In the same way that smokers know cigarettes are bad for them or problem drinkers that alcohol is their downfall, rejected lovers understand that to keep pursuing or holding a candle for someone brings nothing but pain and rejection. However, they just can't stop themselves. So what's the answer?

- **Make a commitment to change.** Some people cling to old love because they believe it shows great strength of character, proof of a 'great love' or because they are secretly enjoying the 'tragedy'. Others believe that they are just 'prisoners' of their feelings and unable to change. Put such destructive thoughts aside and take charge of your destiny.
- **One day at a time.** Instead of worrying about an endless future without your beloved, concentrate on getting through the next twenty-four hours without resorting to self-destructive behaviour (such as phoning, driving past or web-stalking). It takes time but remember the promise at the beginning of this book: It will get better.
- **Keep focused.** It might seem harmless to have a quick peek at your ex's social networking page or to phone one of his or her friends. However, the first step soon turns into an avalanche of regrets, anger and resentment.

So keep yourself safe by being focused and avoiding that first slip.

- **Remove the traps.** Think back to past episodes of destructive behaviour. What has prompted these problems? Had you been drinking or indulging in 'what if' fantasies? How can you avoid such slippery places in future?

- **Think past the bliss.** In the same way that AA encourages alcoholics to think past the pleasure of the first drink and on to the chaos that follows, think past the bliss of seeing or talking to your ex. Imagine his surprise that you're still holding a candle, because he's moved on. Imagine her annoyance, because you've called so many times before. Think about the rejection and how it feeds your cycle of depression.

- **Be positive.** Keep busy with exciting new hobbies or interests. Take plenty of exercise. Develop a positive picture about a future returned love. Where will you and this new person be? What are you doing? Make the picture as detailed as possible. Each time you are tempted to dwell on the past, flash up your positive goal.

# Summing Up

When a relationship has truly broken down, it is better to stop striving for an unrealistic ending and to make a good job of accepting a real one. Although the Leaver normally reaches this stage first, the Sticker will catch up. It helps if you can find a story that explains the break-up and instead of repressing natural emotions – such as anger and depression – work through them. Although there will be slips back to Crisis and Adjustment, over time, you will be hopeful for longer periods and more secure in Acceptance.

## NUTSHELLS FOR LEAVERS:

- Remember your partner will take longer to get here.
- Sometimes fighting with your partner – over who is to blame for the split, money or the children – binds the two of you together and makes the parting harder.
- Keep your partner informed of new developments in your life, so that he or she doesn't hear about them from someone else – as this will only increase their pain.

**NUTSHELLS FOR STICKERS:**

- Although it is difficult to let go, there comes a time when fighting to save your relationship only prolongs the pain.
- Accepting the inevitable is hard but it is like a huge weight slipping off your back.
- Closing the door on your relationship will open a window on to a better future.

STEP 5

# HELPING THE CHILDREN

When I lay out the seven steps to heal and move on for clients who have children, I put step four, Acceptance, and step five, Helping the Children, side by side.

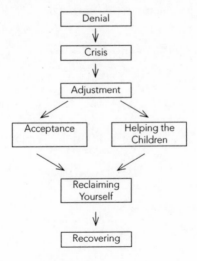

In a sense, it is impossible to fully accept a break-up until the children have been informed and helped over the worst of the fallout.

When I drew the diagram on the previous page for Donald, he put a cross just above Acceptance. So what was holding him back from setting a date when he and Deborah would tell the children? 'I suppose, that would make it real,' he confessed. 'Deborah would tell them tomorrow. In fact, she's so impatient she said, "Tell them what you like. Blame me. I don't care," but I just can't face it.' To help Donald prepare, we went through the following form and headings so that he could discuss the issues with his wife and mentally prepare for talking to his children.

## JOINT MESSAGE

Top line:

What this means practically:

Why:

Mission Statement:

## INDIVIDUAL MESSAGE

What I feel:

What I want in the future:

## INDIVIDUAL MESSAGE

What I feel:

What I want in the future:

For Donald, the top line of the joint message was: *We are going to split*. Fortunately, in the short term, the practical implications were not huge: *Until we can sell the house, I will still be living here. However, we're no longer going to be sharing a bedroom*. For reasons why: *We got married very young. We have grown apart and want different things*. For the mission statement, he wrote: *Treat each other with respect*. (This was particularly important for Donald because he felt Deborah ran down his efforts – such as preparing a cooked Sunday breakfast for the children.) I balanced this out by suggesting: *We will not blame each other*.

Moving on to the second part, the Individual Message, it is unlikely that you and your partner will have matching statements. However, it is better to discuss these issues openly with your partner than to fight covertly through the children. If your messages are very contradictory, it could be that you and your partner need to spend more time talking and making adjustments. (You could also consider using the mediation services offered at most Relate centres or contact the Family Mediators Association.) When Donald did this exercise, his individual message to the children was: *I didn't want us to split up. I love you. I want us to have a better relationship in the future. Although I'm going to have a demanding time at work, I am committed to giving quality time to you.*

Here are some important issues to consider:

- Where will your children live?
- What school will they attend?
- What about pets?
- What arrangements will be taken for seeing each parent?
- What about seeing friends, relatives and other significant people?
- What will you tell the school?

- How can we keep as much stability as possible, especially in the first few weeks and months, when the children are only starting to process the information?

## What Goes Wrong?

Every couple agrees to put the interests of their children first but many fall at the first hurdle. So how could you avoid the sort of angry scenes which make a break-up worse for children?

### Criticising the other parent

However justified you might feel, criticising your partner just invites him or her to criticise you back. Before too long, you are retaliating and the argument spirals into anger and bitterness. 'I just "mentioned" that he shouldn't send the children back burdened down with sweets and toys after every access visit,' said Tara, twenty-nine. 'But he laid in about how I'd stopped them coming the weekend before – but our youngest had a birthday party that she couldn't be expected to miss.' Not only does this sort of argument not address the real underlying issues (guilt, fear and settling scores) but it didn't solve Tara's specific worry: spoiling the children. So what's the alternative? First, wait twenty-four hours before tackling any issue. Once the anger has dissipated, the problem might have disappeared too. Second, instead of criticising, initiate a general debate about your concerns – for example, 'I am worried about the amount of sweets that the children are eating; could we come to some agreement?' Look for points of agreement rather than exposing disagreements.

## Fear

Although we continue to love our children unconditionally and unselfishly, the break-up of our relationship with our partner reminds us that some other kinds of love are not always unconditional or selfless. So it is not surprising that we become anxious about all forms of love and fear losing our children's love too. This is what makes us competitive or jealous of our partner. When Tara did talk to her husband, Peter, about the last access visit, he opened up about his anxiety: 'I thought that if I didn't give them a wonderful time, I'd be at a disadvantage because they're with you all the time. It's stupid, really, because I don't want them to become spoilt brats who feel entitled to everything they want.'

## Settling scores

It takes work, time and self-knowledge to recover from a relationship break-up. Unfortunately, some people plunge into the future without going through Adjustment and Acceptance and therefore carry a lot of bitterness with them. With none of the old fights resolved, the only continuing point of contact – the children – becomes the new arena to score points.

'If I didn't get my daughter back on the dot,' explained Scott, 'Victoria would go off the deep end, but I don't want to spend my special day with her constantly looking at my watch. It's my time and, within reason, I should be able to bring her back when it suits me.'

Victoria, of course, saw things differently: 'Our daughter needs her routine. Not Daddy bringing her back at all hours and being tired and grumpy the next day. If I phone and ask where they are, Scott gets all huffy and hangs up.' Unfortunately, neither partner was prepared to budge and their arguments moved from timekeeping to the amount of access. The best way to lower the temperature is to understand the next point.

## Projection

We identify so closely with our children that we project all our hopes and fears on to them. Unfortunately, at times of stress and crisis, we tend to convince ourselves that our needs and theirs are one and the same. Returning to Donald and Deborah, he saw their impending split as disastrous (and therefore maximised the harm to their five children) while Deborah was itching to be free (and therefore minimised the impact). In reality, the truth would be somewhere in between their two views. Unfortunately, for some couples, the projection is so strong that the partners not only exaggerate the evidence that supports their viewpoint but also close their eyes to any contrary evidence. Therefore, convinced by their own rightness, they pump up their fears, hopes and point-scoring and remain oblivious to their children's true feelings. If this sounds familiar, step back and ask yourself: What do I want? What do my children want? It is seldom exactly the same thing.

## CHALLENGE TOXIC THOUGHTS

Having a balanced view of the split will not only encourage your partner to be more balanced too, but will also help your children adjust to their new life. So taking the most important regrets about your split, ask yourself the following questions:

- Have I overestimated my responsibility (and therefore increased my feelings of guilt)?
- Have I denied my responsibility?
- Is there any false blame?
- Have I made the past seem very black and white without contradictions, paradoxes and ambiguities?
- Did I assume superhero skills – such as second sight or a super-smooth tongue to persuade someone to change?
- Am I expecting an apology from my partner or to be vindicated? (This is not only wishful thinking but it also pumps up our anger or expectations.)

## What Should We Tell the Children?

Your relationship with your partner might be ending but your responsibilities as co-parents go on for ever. Start as you mean to go on by talking to your children together (rather than turning them into confidants) and all at the same time (so no child is left holding a secret). What you say should be tailored to your children's ages, personalities and how many of your problems they have witnessed:

## Pre-school

- These children are totally dependent on their parents and will naturally fear being abandoned.
- At this age, children do not understand the link between cause and effect, so they will draw conclusions that adults find bizarre – the most common is that their naughtiness caused their parents' divorce.
- Remember that in their minds, they have 'lost' one parent and therefore another could simply disappear.
- Give them plenty of reassurance and understanding if they have trouble letting you out of their sight.
- Keep checking as they get older that they are still not holding on to childish conclusions about the reasons for your divorce.

## Early school – five to eight

- Children have a right to understand what is after all a major – if not *the* major – crisis in their childhood.
- Until they understand what is going on, they will find it hard to cope.
- Present your divorce as a solution that you have come to reluctantly only after exploring all the other options.
- In effect, you are presenting them with an important model: you have made a serious mistake, you have tried to rectify it and, finally, you are pursuing a moral and socially responsible remedy.
- Keep your children posted on all the major developments and keep checking back about how they are doing.

## Nine plus

- Children feel powerless after a divorce.
- Therefore it is important to consult them over minor issues – especially over matters that directly affect them – and to make certain that their suggestions are taken seriously.
- However, they should not be made to feel responsible for major decisions.

## Adolescence

- Divorce heightens the normal fears of adolescents: Who am I? How do I fit in? How am I going to make my way in the world?
- Children of divorce need extra support at this time.
- Find a way to cooperate with your former spouse to arrive at a consistent set of rules that can be applied in all circumstances. Adolescents need clear boundaries and are most likely to play one parent off against another.
- Be prepared to seek help and advice from other parents and professionals.

## For all children

- Give them permission to love both parents.
- Offer continuous reassurance that it is not their fault.
- Honesty is incredibly important. If you don't know the answer, be up-front and commit to sharing information as and when the situation becomes clearer.
- Look out for changes in their behaviour. Are they taking out their anger and frustration in an inappropriate manner? Are they coping

better than you could ever have expected? (This is probably a sign that they are repressing difficult feelings.)

- Provide them with the opportunity to discuss the impact on their lives and ask questions – and not just in the immediate aftermath of the split.
- Understand that divorce is a continuing presence in their life that needs different approaches at different ages.

## MONEY AND CHILDREN

Beyond the formal agreement about child support and maintenance, there are lots of smaller financial issues that can cause parents to fall out. Here are some topics to discuss: *Who will pay for the children's . . .*

- Clothes and shoes?
- Uniforms, sporting equipment and kit?
- Transport costs to see each of you or relatives and friends?
- School trips?
- Pocket money?
- Larger items – like computers, bicycles and musical instruments?

# The Long Picture

Although there are plenty of horror stories about the impact of divorce on children, it does not have to be this way. Adrian is thirty-two and recently had a child with his long-term partner. He remembers the day his parents told him about their split as a loving family occasion: 'I was about seven or eight and we were all on holiday in the South of France. One morning, they asked us to come into their room and the three of us children sat on the bed and they told us: "We have some news. Mum has fallen in love with Uncle Mick [friend of the family] and they have decided to live together. Dad is fine with it. We still love each other but we'd be happier like this."

'We were all quite stoic about it. I remember thinking: If they're happier, that's fine. My sister, who was four years younger, wanted to know about Sandra [Mick's wife]. She needed to logically work it out in her head as she was the only person in the foursome that they hadn't talked about.'

Fortunately, there was little upheaval. 'My parents had moved to South Africa and I'd been sent back to England to boarding school. I enjoyed boarding school, I enjoyed going to South Africa, and Mum came back to England with Mick and lived near to my and my brother's school. So this way, I saw more of her.'

Adrian's parents continued to cooperate throughout his childhood. 'We would do these swap-overs at various service stations. Mum would drive halfway and so would Dad. There was no acrimony. They would chat.' It was in marked contrast with Mick and Sandra's handover with their children, which Adrian often witnessed. 'There was a black cloud. Sandra was very cross, bitter and full of resentment. She wouldn't get out of the car. Later, I learned, my stepbrother and stepsister wouldn't talk about what they had done with us because Sandra would get very jealous or throw tantrums – especially if we'd been on a nice holiday together.'

So what made Adrian's experience of divorce a positive one? 'My parents never stopped loving each other. My mum took her vows very seriously. She didn't go to church for ten years after getting divorced. She would have stayed married to Dad if she'd felt her level of commitment was reciprocated.'

Like many children of divorce, Adrian is very thoughtful. He has also found a very balanced picture of his parents. 'I don't think it was because

Dad wasn't in love with Mum but because he had a strange childhood and didn't know how to show his feelings.' In his mid-twenties, Adrian needed to really understand the break-up. 'I confronted my dad and asked if he'd had affairs. He told me: "Don't be ridiculous, your mother had the affair." I pressed him. Are you sure? Did you at any time sleep with anybody else? He replied: "Obviously with hookers, but then everybody did that on business trips in the seventies." I don't think he felt entirely blameless and that helped him understand where Mum was coming from.'

Research into the long-term impact of acrimonious divorces shows the children of these marriages find it harder to trust when they grow up and make long-term relationships. Adrian's stepbrother, for example, has not got married. 'He doesn't really have girlfriends. He is very shy around women.' Adrian himself is also in two minds about marriage: 'I've never felt any great need, but I think it would add a new dimension to my relationship. But my partner's parents are also divorced and she has a bitter mother who tried to turn her against her father. So she's never been that keen on marriage. Although, since the birth of our baby, she has started to want it much more. It's about getting into the right space in my head and finding the right time to ask.'

So what can you learn from Adrian that could benefit your children? First, his parents were far enough out of the Crisis stage to offer a united front when telling their children. Second, they kept disruption to a minimum. However, most importantly, they didn't fight through their children – even though Adrian's father could have seen himself having 'just cause'. Finally, they continued to answer their children's questions – many years after the first announcement – in an open and honest way.

## Summing Up

Although your focus is on telling your children about your separation and managing the immediate repercussions, this is only the beginning of a lifetime of cooperating with your ex-partner. Even if there has been long-term unhappiness in your home, your children will probably be in denial about the seriousness of the problems and will have to make adjustments before reaching acceptance. They will also be constructing a story in their heads about the reasons for the divorce.

Make certain that they don't think that they are to blame. Present as united a picture as possible, as this will lay the groundwork for allowing your children to continue to love both of you. In many ways, your children are on the same journey to recovery as you are. Remember how long it took you to reach this stage and don't expect too much too soon.

### NUTSHELLS FOR LEAVERS:

- In your determination to move on, don't forget that your children will need time to process the news.
- Allow your children to mourn and don't be afraid to show your own regrets about the split.
- Be aware that the emotional implications of divorce might not emerge for some time after the legal implications have been settled.

## NUTSHELLS FOR STICKERS:

- Acting out your anger about your partner is not good for your children and it won't make you feel better, either.
- If you cry too often in front of your children, they are more likely to suppress their feelings for fear of burdening you.
- Divorce does not necessarily damage children. Many grow up to be thoughtful and more emotionally aware adults.

STEP 6

# RECLAIMING
# YOURSELF

Falling in love takes two separate individuals and turns them into one couple; this next stage – Reclaiming Yourself – reverses the process. Instead of automatically saying: 'I'm not certain if *we* can make it', you have to stop and remember that you're flying solo. Instead of: 'We don't go to the cinema very often', you have to start thinking about your individual tastes. Instead of shared interests and a shared social life, you can do what you want without feeling guilty.

Reclaiming yourself goes deeper than the undisputed possession of the TV remote control. Back at the start of your relationship, you shared out the jobs. So, ending a relationship, you take back responsibilities previously given to your ex. Sometimes this unhooking can be the source of joy – especially if your partner, for example, has done all the cooking and you get a chance to rediscover your culinary skills. Sometimes this is a time of growth: for example, your partner took care of all the money issues and you decide it is time to learn yourself. (For jobs that you cannot do yourself – and have no wish to learn – it is better to ask a friend or hire an expert than to phone your ex-partner. This last option will keep you bound to the old relationship, rather than striking out towards the future.)

After years of compromises and sacrifice, you are finally able to remember who you were before you met your partner. For many people, this can feel like a cloud lifting. Finally, my promise at the start of the book – 'it will get better' – is beginning to come true. In fact, this step feels so much better than the previous ones that some people try and skip through them and reach step six too quickly.

## Double-check that You Are Truly Ready to Reclaim Yourself

Here is a chance to look back at how far you have come and to start making the necessary adjustments for being single again. I have illustrated the process with an example from my casebook:

## 1. Find an explanation for the relationship ending

Graham, twenty-six, had been constantly obsessing about why his girlfriend of four years had split up with him, taken him back, cheated on him, and finally finished the relationship for the second time. The pain had become so bad that, he told me, 'I could drive off a cliff just to get away from it.' Throughout our session, he kept coming back to the same question: 'How could she do it to me?' Especially as he believed: 'I did everything to make her happy.' It became clear that until we could answer this central question, Graham was stuck.

The background between Graham and his girlfriend, Martina, could not have been more contrasting. His parents had been happily married for almost thirty years. Her father had been an alcoholic and her mother had mental health issues. Graham's grandmother summed up the situation very neatly: 'Lovely girl, but can't bring herself to settle down.' Martina's most revealing comment about their relationship was to Graham's mum: 'The bubble is going to burst.' Although his mum tried to reassure her that her son was 'not like that', Martina's life experience told her something different. If Martina's baseline was mildly pessimistic, Graham's was wildly optimistic: 'I could see what she could be.'

After much discussion, Graham decided that the relationship ended because 'we wanted different things'. Contrasting her casual infidelity with his fierce loyalty, he finally admitted: 'We had different values.' From this point onwards, when Graham found himself worrying about the relationship, for example asking: 'Why was it always me who would text first to say "I love you"' – he had a built-in answer. This allowed him to deal quickly with random thoughts about his ex, rather than spiralling down into obsession or depression.

## 2. Give yourself time

Nobody wants to accept this ingredient for healing. We all want to put the pain behind us as quickly as possible; surely a weekend should be enough? Unfortunately, recovery always takes longer than we expect. Graham needed ten months to find enough distance to understand his relationship with Martina properly. Like a lot of people who had been through a painful break-up, Graham had dated someone for a few weeks. Fortunately, he recognised that he was not really interested in this new girl, although she was keen, and he ended the relationship. Not only is it unfair to use someone else as a temporary 'feel good' fix or as a 'security' blanket, but also the inevitable second break-up will bring even more pain. Looking back over twenty-five years of counselling people through break-ups, the cases with the most debilitating pain involve someone throwing themselves into a rebound relationship. The inevitable crash seems to triple the sense of failure, isolation and depression from the first break-up.

## 3. Check and double-check that enough time has passed

Obviously there are no hard-and-fast rules as to when you are ready for a new partner. It depends on both the length and seriousness of your previous relationship. However, in general, I advise waiting a year. There is something very therapeutic about passing all the important anniversaries: first birthday alone, their birthday, Christmas, etc. If you are having trouble coping, or are not good at waiting, look at what you have learned. No experience, however wretched, feels quite so bad if you can find something positive. Graham was startled when I asked him about the benefits of his break-up but, with a little prompting, he came up with four answers: he had got to know himself better; he would take future relationships more slowly; he had become stronger; and finally, he would stop letting people take advantage of him. As Graham admitted: 'I will often do something for somebody else, even if it doesn't fit in with my plans.' Previously, for example, he had been very happy to collect people for away squash matches – even though it never seemed to be his turn to be offered a lift. With this knowledge, Graham found a more equitable arrangement with his squash team. Admittedly, he would much rather have had Martina than these personal insights, but Graham had begun to transform his picture of the past and put down foundations for his future.

## 4. Bring new things into your life

If you keep on doing the same old things, you will have the same old life. Starting new interests or pastimes has two clear benefits: first, it provides a temporary uplift and second, it fills time which could otherwise have been spent obsessing about an ex. Relationships are very time-consuming and one of the worst side effects of a break-up is the loneliness of endless empty weekends. Rather than making late-night drunken phone calls to a former lover, or starting a new 'comfort' relationship, fill the gap with something positive. Graham had already begun to learn to ride a motorbike and used his Sundays for long rides. He also decided to start playing the guitar. Before starting my programme, he had not seen these interests as part of his recovery. Neither motorbikes nor guitars are likely routes for meeting women, but this is just the point. These interests are just for you. Something you have always wanted to do but have not had the time or money for before. In this way, you will be nurturing yourself rather than rushing around looking for someone to provide the quick fix of a new romantic relationship.

## 5. Learn when to listen to the voice in your head and when to distract yourself

Even with an explanation for your break-up and incorporating the other 'moving on' steps, you will still be ambushed by thoughts about your ex. Graham was making good progress and had certainly stopped wallowing in the past. However, he arrived at our fourth session complaining that he had spent most of the week thinking about Martina. None of his usual distraction techniques – like going for a motorbike ride – had worked. In these circumstances, I normally find that the internal voice is there for a reason. In other words, it is trying to tell us something – unfortunately, the message is normally overwhelmed by a lot of over-analysing.

As we talked about the week, Graham explained that Martina's mother had died. He had been trying to decide whether to text his condolences to Martina or not. What would happen if he did? If she texted back, it would just open up the old wounds and if she did not reply, he would be depressed. So Graham decided to do nothing. So I probed further: was there anything else? He was worried that Martina might have a few drinks on Saturday night, get maudlin and call him. (This was how they had got back together after their first break-up.) What were his options? He decided to switch off his mobile on Saturday night. Graham's internal voice had, indeed, good reason for communicating. For advice on sorting out the important questions from just obsessing, see the exercise opposite.

# HOW TO LISTEN EFFECTIVELY TO YOUR INNER VOICE

## 1. Write down everything

As the thoughts pop up, write them down: no censorship, however ludicrous. Don't try to answer anything, just move on to the next thought. This is what Graham came up with when I led him through this exercise in one of our sessions:

- Why sleep with someone else?
- How can she be so nasty?
- How can she blame me?
- How can you say you love someone and not mean it?
- Why say something like . . . I didn't used to love you but I love you now?
- Can I ever trust someone again?
- Can I ever talk to someone again?
- How can I have the same feelings for someone?
- All I want is to be happy.
- I used to be so easygoing.

## 2. Turn statements into questions

Sentences like 'All I want is to be happy' and 'I used to be so easygoing' encourage us to feel stuck and hopeless. Instead, turn them into questions:

- How can I be happy?
- How can I be easygoing again?

Immediately, we have a task and can begin to look for solutions. The second benefit is that you will no longer feel passive or a prisoner of your feelings.

### 3. Go back and start answering the questions

Now the questions are on paper, rather than going round in your head, they are more manageable. Certainly, Graham found he could answer, in seconds, what had been troubling him for hours. His answers follow the questions.

- Why sleep with someone else? *She wanted to and didn't think about me.*
- How can she be so nasty? *It is easy to blame someone else for your bad behaviour.*
- How can she blame me? *See above.*
- How can you say you love someone and not mean it? *Just words.*
- Why say something like . . . I didn't used to love you but I love you now? *See above.*
- Can I ever trust someone again? *Yes.*
- Can I ever talk to someone again? *Yes.*
- How can I have the same feelings for someone? *I don't know but I hope I can.*

## 4. Some questions will need greater thought

Often underneath all the worry about the relationship ending will be larger questions that tap into larger issues.

In Graham's case they were:

1. How can I be happy?
2. How can I be easygoing again?

Graham had answered the previous questions almost spontaneously. These final two took greater thought. Eventually he came up with the following.

1. *Riding my motorbike. I will meet someone else someday.*
2. *There are times when it is OK to lose my patience. It is part of not letting people take advantage of me.*

If you need help, try phoning a friend to talk it over. A lot of people are reluctant to ask for more help, fearing that they have already bored friends by endlessly talking about their ex. However, there is a big difference between rambling on about the past and tightly targeted questions like these.

# Reclaiming After a Shorter-term Relationship

Although the recovery process after a relationship breaks down is the same whether you and your ex were together for six months, six years or sixty years, there are different challenges along the way. If you and your partner have been together a shorter time, it is likely that you will reach Acceptance more quickly. If there are no children born from your partnership, you can not only skip stage five altogether but also have the option of making a clean break. On the surface, stage six – Reclaiming Yourself – should be relatively simple. After all, it is not that long ago that you were single. However, many people have recovered from past relationships not by healing and moving on, but by jumping straight into a new relationship. In some cases, there is even a small overlap between one relationship 'officially' ending and the next beginning. So although these people have not been married or lived with their partner – and considered themselves single – there has always been someone in their lives or in the wings. Under these circumstances, it is particularly difficult to answer the questions: Who am I? What do I want? What do

I need? Without this knowledge, it is particularly hard to reclaim yourself.

Instead of looking for a new man or woman, and risking taking all the old baggage into a new relationship, spend some time reflecting and doing a relationship detox.

1. To take stock, select a picture of each person that you have had a serious relationship with and spread them out in front of you. At first sight each of your 'ex files' will seem very different. Most people don't have a type and will have dated people with different looks, jobs and backgrounds. The secret is to uncover the underlying similarities. Here are some common themes:

- **Extreme dating.** Your ex-lovers were all difficult but you enjoyed the challenge or drama of never knowing what to expect from them.
- **Comfort dating.** They wrapped you in cotton wool and admired you greatly but, ultimately, they bored you.
- **Trophy dates.** They impressed your friends but ultimately there was no chemistry.
- **Wounded birds.** These dates brought out your protective side and made you feel strong, needed or important.

- **Knights or ladies in shining armour.** They promised to solve your problems or look after you but ended up being controlling.
- **Social dating.** You might have liked your date, but the real meeting of minds was with his or her family, children or network of friends.

Be aware that going for the opposite type is not moving on; it is, normally, playing the same dilemma from a different angle. For example: if you have been cheated on in one relationship, playing fast and loose in the next.

2. What issues keep on coming up over and over again? Is there something that your dating history might be trying to tell you? Rather than jumping into the relationship – and possibly acting out the same problems again – is there another way of tackling these issues?

3. Avoid dating for between three and six months – depending on how stuck you feel. This is especially important if you have a low opinion of yourself. Use the time to repair the damage. This could be reading self-help books, going on a retreat or taking an adult education course. Consider doing some

voluntary work. Offering to fix the guttering for an elderly neighbour or volunteering for a kids' adventure training holiday will not only divert your attention from your own problems but, also, the praise and thanks will make you feel better.

4. Finally, break the general patterns: seek new hobbies and interests, go out with different mates or simply change your route to work.

## BE PHILOSOPHICAL
Whether we realise it or not, everyone has their own personal philosophy that underpins their life. These philosophies are central to our view of the world and ourselves – so central, in fact, that they are often unspoken, unexamined and untested. This is a pity because a well-balanced personal philosophy is the key to feeling happy and fulfilled. What is yours?

1. You're waiting to hear about a perfect job, but they are taking longer than expected to let you know. Do you:
   a) Phone all your contacts to find out what's going on;

b) Do nothing: if it's meant to be, it's meant to be;

c) Wait patiently: I'll find out soon enough?

2. You have a new boss at work and the two of you don't click. You feel picked on, stressed and unhappy. Do you:

a) Start looking for another job;

b) Hope the problems will sort themselves;

c) Speak to someone in human resources?

3. Your relationship ended three months ago and your confidence is in pieces. What is your attitude?

a) Get back out there: I'll show him/her I'm better off without them.

b) How could he/she?

c) It'll take time to get over my wounds but I'll make it.

4. You went out with a new prospect whom you really liked. He or she promised to call but you've waited five days and heard nothing. Do you:

a) Phone him or her;

b) Keeping checking your phone for messages, texts and check your emails almost hourly;

c) Think: I've better things to do?

5. You've been seeing someone for six to nine months and although it started well, there are problems and you're anxious that the relationship is about to collapse. Do you:
   a) Get in quick and end it first;
   b) Worry and try desperately to please;
   c) Accept that it might end and then start finding ways to sort it out?

6. When it comes to a holiday in an exotic or unknown destination, which statement best describes your attitude?
   a) I get peace of mind by researching the place in advance and tie down all the details so I know exactly what to expect.
   b) Leave the arrangements to the friend with whom I'm going on holiday.
   c) The adventure is part of the fun.

## Mostly a): Control freak

There is nothing more unsettling for you than not knowing. You would much rather be doing something – anything – even if it's wrong. Deep down you feel that love is a test that you either pass or fail. However, you need to grasp that we can't control every single aspect of our lives. Once you can truly accept this truth, both intellectually and emotionally, you will be free to enjoy life more. Next time you feel compelled to act, put everything on hold for forty-eight hours. In most cases, you will find there was no need to do anything.

## Mostly b): Passive acceptance

You hate to rock the boat and would rather do nothing than risk making the wrong move. On a positive note: you have truly accepted that we cannot control every aspect of our lives. Well done. However, you often cling so tightly to your expectation of how something should turn out that you fail to notice other opportunities or new doors opening. Finally, stick up for yourself. It is often the first step to solving a problem, rather than just side-stepping it.

## Mostly c): Embracing the unknown

When faced with uncertainty, you do your best and let the rest go. In effect, you have learned to live with the three most difficult human emotions: I call them the triple A: anxiety, ambivalence, ambiguity. This is a hard path to tread and if you feel yourself panicking, talk over your problems with a friend. Sometimes it takes an outside eye to know the difference between what can be changed and what is beyond our control.

# Raising Your Self-esteem

It is difficult to reclaim yourself if you don't particularly like yourself. The following will help redress the balance:

## 1. Building on firm foundations

Get a piece of paper and write down *one* thing under the following headings and then add beside it *one* thing that your best friend might write. Finally add *one* thing that an ethical advertising agency might use to write a contact advert for you or a letter applying for a job. As this is an ethical advertising agency, they can exaggerate but will never tell lies.

- An attractive part of my body
- A valuable aspect of my personality
- A past achievement
- An aspect of untapped potential

If you can't come up with something for one of the headings, don't worry, as this exercise will take some time. Put the paper to one side and ask your best friend to help. The ethical advertising agency will be the hardest but trust that the ideas will come and, when you least expect it, they will pop into your head. Ultimately, you will have twelve compliments to boost your self-confidence.

## 2. What one thing would you like to change about yourself?

Close your eyes and really picture what life would be like if you got it. What would you see? How would it feel? Expand the picture and walk around in it. What can you smell? What can you taste? What can you hear? What can you touch? Indulge all your senses.

## 3. How can you make this happen?

First of all make sure that your goal is framed as a positive. For example, instead of 'stop being shy', reframe it as 'I want to be happy talking in front of strangers'. Next ask yourself: 'How will I know when I have achieved this?' It could be 'When I speak up at a meeting at work' or 'When I ask a question at a public lecture/talk'. Once you have a goal, ask yourself: 'How can I go about it?' For example, reading the agenda for the next staff meeting so that you are fully prepared, or researching an author who is coming to your local book festival so you can ask something during the Q&A session. Finally, decide what the first step would be. For example, booking a ticket for the talk or volunteering to be co-opted on to a committee at work.

## 4. Reward yourself

Every time you make a small step on the road to your goal, make a note of your achievement and give yourself a reward. It could be a piece of chocolate, spending Sunday morning in bed, watching a movie, or treating yourself to a gadget or some other luxury. However, it is important to celebrate your successes.

# Identifying Your 'Reclaiming' Goals

To help understand your challenge for this stage, look at the diagram on the next page and think about how you and your partner divided up the jobs, tasks and responsibilities on a regular basis.

| Me | My Partner |
|---|---|
|  |  |

When I did this exercise with Donald, whose progress we've followed through the book, he put very little down for his side. 'Go to work and earn the money', 'Cut the grass', 'Sort out practical problems', 'Plumbing' and 'Wiring'. For Deborah's side: 'Bringing up kids', 'Looking after the kids', 'Sorting out finances', 'Cooking', 'Gardening', 'Making decisions', 'Supervising my relationship with my mother', 'Buying presents', 'Buying clothes for me', 'Craft work', 'Business side of life: speaking to solicitors, bank managers, etc.' and 'Emotional life'.

If there is something that belongs on both sides, you can either put it in both columns or write it over the middle. Donald put 'Renovating houses' in this category as he and Deborah had done up and sold three. 'All I did was go to work and then come home and work on the house. We had no social life or friends,' he explained. So this was your bond? I asked. 'Perhaps that was part of the problem,' he answered. 'I got fed up with Deborah making all the decisions on the house and slowly withdrew until we did nothing together.'

The challenge is to take as many items from your partner's side of the table and start doing them yourself. So how much progress had Donald made? 'I bought a football shirt for my son's birthday – even though Deborah said he only wanted money – and he was really pleased. I cleaned the bathroom, because it was in a terrible state. I've started buying my own clothes and exploring my own tastes – which I'm looking forward to doing more of. I've been cooking for the kids and started taking responsibility for leisure by taking golf lessons.' In effect, he had made a good start to reclaiming himself. 'But I'm aware that I've only been taking tiny footsteps and I don't want to rush headlong into a new relationship.' Donald was very sensible. If you do not complete 'Reclaiming Yourself', you risk repeating the same dynamic again. 'That would be like crossing Deborah's name out and putting someone else's there,' he said in a moment of reflection.

Frederick, from Chapter One, whose wife continued her affair and lied about it during their counselling, wrote again to my website: 'Over the seven months prior to separating, I was very much in love with my wife and was putting in all the effort to get the relationship back on track but my wife wasn't able to bring herself to try. I feel that I've reached the acceptance stage but am I deluding myself? Two weeks after separating from my wife – although still living under the same roof – I got talking to someone on the phone about a business issue and we clicked straight away. We have been emailing each other for the last week or so and have arranged to meet for coffee. She hasn't asked about my relationship status. I want to be open and honest with her but how do I tell her my situation (I look after my three-year-old son for four days a week and have just amicably separated) without scaring her off?' Frederick might have reached Acceptance but until he has reclaimed himself, any new relationship would be tangled up in the old.

## BRINGING NEW THINGS INTO YOUR LIFE

The end of a relationship brings lots of holes into your life. If you have an all-consuming hobby, enjoy sports or have a drive to help in the community, it is reasonably easy to meet new people. If this is not you, this exercise will help fill the holes, uncover fresh challenges and explore the emerging new you:

1. **Remember your childhood.** Children love to play, it is how they discover their skills and their creative abilities. Unfortunately, as we get older, we begin to censor ourselves. 'I will never play football for Manchester United' or 'I will never dance a solo for the Royal Ballet'. What would you have done if only you had had the opportunity, the encouragement or the self-belief? If you find it hard to remember, ask your parents or look at old home movies. When I did this exercise myself, during a time of crisis, I remembered my childhood desire to have a puppy which ultimately led to getting a collie/spaniel cross and joining a dog agility club.

2. **What makes you angry?** There is passion in anger and creativity too. It might be that there is nothing for young people in your area. Perhaps the suffering of animals or cancer patients gets you going. Then research which charities are looking for volunteers.

3. **Switch off your television on three consecutive evenings.** The TV not only swallows hours

of our spare time but acts like a tranquilliser and stops us thinking. Although the first evening will probably be uncomfortable, these are the withdrawal symptoms – stick with it. (Try not to use other distraction tactics – like going into Internet chat-rooms.) By the second evening, you will be calmer and other ways to occupy yourself will suggest themselves. Even if these do not seem very promising, do not be discouraged. Even something physical, like scrubbing the kitchen floor, can occupy the body and allow the unconscious to throw out some good ideas. By the third evening, you will probably have some ideas to research. Follow these threads of interest and see where they go.

4. **Think outside the box.** Don't be put off by big ideas. In fact, the bigger the better. At the dreaming stage, you can do anything. So don't shut down a potential avenue by getting all practical, allow your imagination to float free. Wait until your passion is firmly established before looking at how to turn an idea into a reality. OK, you will not be playing for Manchester United, but you could train to be a referee or coach a youth team. Want to get into films? Although you are unlikely to cause

Nicole Kidman any sleepless nights, you could register with an agency that provides extras for film and TV productions.

5. **What is stopping you?** Write down all the excuses and look at them rationally. Are they valid? Ask yourself: Am I exaggerating? Should they really stop me from pressing ahead?

## Closure

Several of my clients arrive seeking something called 'closure'. After the first time it was mentioned, I consulted my dictionaries of psychological and psychoanalytical terms but found nothing. I was surprised. Where had this term come from? It is neither a medical nor a religious concept – the other main sources for psychological-sounding words that enter the general vocabulary. Closure, the idea that we can somehow deal with a past painful relationship, package it up and move on, is such a seductive idea that we have invented our own word and now want to believe in it. But is it possible?

When someone is determined to reach closure, I am sympathetic but always probe deeper. Some clients hope to skip some of the pain by rationalising and packing it away. Although this process can help, it is not a magic bullet. Other clients have used closure as the cover for some pretty nasty behaviour. Hannah had been having an affair with a married man for three years: 'I had no choice but to go round and tell his wife. She had a right to know and how else was I going to achieve closure?' This is dramatic, but never final. The confrontation just launches another round of recriminations. Indeed, Hannah's boyfriend turned up on her doorstep and started shouting at her. 'It was not at all healing,' she admitted.

Ultimately, the best way forward is to repackage the pain into something positive. I helped Hannah look back at her painful parting as the moment she started painting pictures. Another client remembered how his former lover had introduced him to meditation. Even bad relationships teach us something. If this does not work for you, take a long hard look at the benefits of staying where you are. This seems mad, because who would want to keep hurting? But, sometimes, it feels safer to cling on to a failed relationship than face our fears: 'I'll never find anyone else to love me,' or 'I can't cope with the loneliness.'

Be as honest with yourself as possible and keep digging deeper. Once everything is out in the open, the underlying assumptions can be properly challenged, anxieties chopped down to size, and a way forward found.

Finally, be patient with yourself. A relationship break-up is as traumatic as a bereavement, so never underestimate what you have been through. Congratulate yourself on your progress so far and be assured that the pain will lessen over time. Although, ultimately, we may never achieve complete closure, we can integrate the past into a better future.

## Summing Up

Falling in love is wonderful but it means submerging part of our identity into a new couple identity. Ending a relationship involves not only rediscovering the old you but incorporating the lessons learned from being a couple and forging a brand-new identity. If this process is rushed, there is a danger of repeating the old patterns all over again with someone new.

**NUTSHELLS FOR LEAVERS:**

- Moving on is more complicated than just ending the relationship.
- It takes time to become your own person again and however much you looked forward to this stage, there are no short cuts.
- Make certain you have properly finished one relationship before embarking on a new one.

**NUTSHELLS FOR STICKERS:**

- Finally, you can find some positives in splitting up.
- Don't worry if your partner seems further ahead in coming to terms with the break-up, life is not a race.
- What matters is not how quickly you recover but how well.

STEP 7

# RECOVERING

Recovering from a relationship breakdown – especially one not of your choosing – is hard. In my experience people who swim, rather than sink, have pulled off a difficult trick. They spend enough time on understanding the relationship (the past), but concentrate on changing things for the better (the future); yet, when times are tough, they focus down to the next few days (today). Although the ability to alternate through these three time-frames is useful at any time, it becomes crucial during a personal setback – like a divorce. People who are stuck in the past frame risk depression; while those that set off with their eyes fixed only on the future are most likely to crash and burn. People with problems caused by sticking to today are rarer – most of us find it hard to live in the moment – but occasionally I see clients who are living in the 'present hedonistic' (focused only on feeling good today and becoming trapped in pointless pleasure-seeking) or 'present fatalistic' (just swept along by events). So how can you be flexible enough to find the right time-frame at the right moment? The secret is to understand the advantages of all three.

The future offers the promise of a brighter tomorrow: no more tears, no more pain and maybe even a new partner. Not surprisingly, most people want those goals now and indeed many clients ask: 'Why does everything have to be so hard?' I do not answer, partly because I am not a philosopher but mainly because counselling is about helping people find their own answers. However, if I could fly in an emergency on-call philosopher, he or she would probably answer: 'Because nobody has ever learned anything important from happiness or success; problems make us grow.' Maybe it is just as well these flying philosophers do not exist because they would not be very popular.

An example of adversity teaching us important lessons is Nuala Bingham, who developed a complex viral illness when she was just twenty-nine. Her husband, Harry, had to give up a high-flying city career to nurse her round the clock.

Three years later, when I met them, her energy levels were still so low that she considered it a good day when she could dress herself. She turned out to be one of the wisest people I have ever met: 'When I get very low, I can't go for a run or have a drink like other people. I just have to work on my inner self; there's nowhere else to go. It's a bit like being a Tibetan monk without the Himalayas in the background! I used to think I'd lost everything that makes someone feel worthwhile. Where is my dignity when Harry has to carry me to the bath? But I discovered it is beyond being able to wash yourself. I still feel a human being because that's what I see reflected when I look into Harry's eyes. He still has the same respect and affection.'

Going back to my clients – who ask why life is hard – if the evidence of my flying philosopher and Nuala Bingham do not work, I would probably call Dave Stewart from the pop group the Eurythmics. This talented and rich musician once suffered from Paradise Syndrome. He had panic attacks, which left him paralysed on the floor, simply because he had nothing to worry about! It seems humans need problems because pain provides the building blocks for a better tomorrow.

# Reaching for the Future

Here are two examples from my casebook about moving forward: one of them successful and one less so. Although Alan felt lonely after his fifteen-year marriage ended and despite the fact that he missed his teenage daughter, he decided to concentrate on the opportunities. 'There were two things I'd always wanted to do: flying and dancing. But I didn't have time for either before and, to be frank, my wife discouraged outside interests. Now I've not only enjoyed the new challenges but also met some great people.'

Although Ken had been married for a similar duration as Alan and had children too, his story is quite different: 'My friends told me I was better off without my wife. I didn't believe them, but they took me out drinking and I bet you can guess the rest. I started dating the barmaid, and the beginning was incredible – such a high. Before long, we were talking about living together and planning a holiday in Florida. But I discovered she was seeing someone else too.' Ken took this break-up harder than his wife leaving and he sank into depression. Unfortunately, he had tried to reach his future life too quickly. Ken thought he had found a woman ready for long-term commitment, whereas she had seen their relationship as a bit of fun.

## EMOTIONAL RESCUE PACKAGE

However positive people choose to be, there are always times when the pain comes crowding back. Normally these destructive thoughts come as pictures or short reels of film. For example, you imagine your ex-partner lying back in the bath with a favourite book and a drink. Meanwhile, you still have to cope with the three kids. Alternatively, it might be an event that you regret and your memory keeps playing it over and over. The natural response is to push down these pictures and distract ourselves with something else. Instead, try the following exercise. It works best when you're not likely to be interrupted.

- Changing the picture is the best way of repro-gramming your brain to cope with disaster. Give the picture a headline name. Speak it out loud, as this is the first step to distancing yourself from the pain. (For example, you could call the bath picture: hippo. A bit of humour always helps diffuse pain.)
- Where is the picture in your imagination? (Is it straight in front of your eyes or to one side, or perhaps wrapped all round you?) Be specific. Where could you put it and feel better? Try turning the picture into a movie playing on

the wall. This can make it seem even further away and therefore less painful. Remember the importance of being specific and again try to speak the results out loud.

- What colour is the picture? Sometimes changing your picture from black and white to colour, or vice versa, can help you make a memory or your idea of an ex-partner's new life feel less vivid. It depends on how your imagination works.

- Is it a moving or still picture? What can you hear? Once again, changing the form of the picture or changing the voices (turning their volume down; changing the voice to Mickey Mouse-style, etc.) can change the way the memory is stored. Is there a smell or a taste involved? Could you swap a sad sensation for a happier one?

- Try replaying the movie again. How would you like to change it? (For example, the bath water turns too hot and your ex-partner has to leap out, or the Queen is being shown through his or her bathroom and stops to peer over the tub. She might even ask: 'Have you come far?') By playing around with your fantasy of their new life, you will be reminded that it is only a fantasy. Alternatively imagine the camera pulling back from the bath and seeing the rest of the house and his or her clothes lying all over the place. Now you can feel relieved that you do not have to pick up after him or her any more.

## Finding a New Path

Rather than leaping in with both feet, it is better to consider your next move carefully:

- **Go for what you want rather than what you don't want.** Many people in crisis are very aware of what they don't want. For example: to be lonely. However, goals are much better if they are framed as a positive. So, for example: I want to make new friends.

- **Be as specific as possible.** The clearer the picture of your new life, the easier it is to spot the first steps on the path. So the above example could be: 'I want to make new friends to go to the theatre.' This more specific goal would focus the mind towards finding out if any colleagues at work were interested in theatre and turning them from acquaintances to friends or joining a relevant club.

- **When looking for new opportunities, bring new patterns into your life.** If you always do the same things, your life will always be the same. So start shaking up your routines – it could be something as simple as taking a new way to work and spotting something that starts a new interest.

- **Open yourself up to inspiration.** Go for walks or take some exercise – anything that occupies the body but allows the mind to wander will free an idea to pop from the subconscious into the conscious. Other possible sources include: surrounding yourself with beauty (going to an art gallery or attending a concert), surfing the Internet, tidying away the clutter in your home, doing something that makes you laugh, or asking a friend for advice.

- **Enjoy the steps on the way.** Sometimes we can be so obsessed with achieving a goal that we forget to stop and smell the flowers on the way. Enjoying the journey also avoids the trap of too-rigid goals and missing out on other options that could also bring happiness.

- **Have you got the right goal?** Most people just want to be happy. Unfortunately, happiness can be very elusive, especially for someone who has been through a relationship breakdown and feels that life has kicked them in the teeth. Although hedonistic pleasures (like a good night out) or sensual ones (a new gadget or new clothes) can bring happiness, it tends to be a short-term relief. However, if the goal is to *grow and become a better person*, no experience is wasted.

## BOOST YOUR SELF-CONFIDENCE

If the end of a significant relationship has undermined your self-confidence – or maybe it was never great in the first place – it will take time to get back on to an even keel. The following seven steps, taken gradually, will stop the rot, provide a more balanced picture and aid recovery.

1. **Stop putting yourself down.** It is amazing how many people litter their conversation with phrases like 'this is probably not a good idea' or manage to both arrive somewhere and dismiss themselves with: 'it's only me'. Listen to other people's conversations and gather more examples, then commit to exorcising them from your vocabulary.

2. **Don't compare yourself.** There are always people who seem to find life easy and radiate confidence. You can never know what is really going on in their heads – they might just be a good actor. Conversely, there might even be people who envy you! Ultimately, comparing yourself to others is a dead-end so concentrate on your own journey.

3. **Reframe your thoughts.** Change the negative into something positive. Instead of 'I can't . . .' or 'I won't . . .' (for example, 'trust anyone ever again') substitute 'I choose to . . .' ('spend time with my friends at the moment' or 'take up a foreign language').

4. **Set small and realistic goals.** Change is frightening and fear makes us close up, retreat and consider ourselves a failure. In contrast, small and easily achieved steps bypass fear and help us feel successful.

5. **Be patient.** Nothing of any value is achieved overnight.

6. **Don't give up.** There will always be obstacles. The difference between people who make it and those who fall by the wayside is that the former look for a way round the problem or simply try again.

7. **Accept yourself, warts and all.** Don't confuse confidence with being perfect.

# Rituals

Mankind has always used rituals to mark the seasons; in the same way, we need to mark the end of one phase of our lives and the beginning of another.

## 1. Check the past is in the past

Spend an evening going back over the past months: What have you learned about yourself? What might hold you back? How could you pre-empt these threats?

## 2. Design a ritual

Find something that seems to sum up the past for you. Some clients write an account of what happened, while some readers of my books gather up the paper used for the exercises and burn them. Another strategy is to find something that encapsulates your past and have a ceremonial trip to the council dump. Alternatively, the act can be completely symbolic like holding a helium-filled balloon on top of a hill and imagining that it holds all the pain and then letting it go. Other cleansing ideas could be making paper boats and sailing them over a weir or casting petals into the wind. The only limit is your imagination.

## 3. Honour the ritual

If you are writing a letter, or an account of your pain, make certain that you do it properly and don't just scribble it on the back of an envelope. Find a location that speaks to you. I had a client who burnt some old pictures on the beach – because she had happy childhood memories there – and watched the tide come in and wash away the ashes. Some clients have chosen poetry and others have even brought music. This all helps to make it a solemn occasion and to add significance. If, for practical reasons, the location is rather ordinary – like the council dump – find somewhere nice to go for a walk or a drink afterwards.

## 4. Celebrate the new

Just as marriage needs witnesses, so does a new life. Some people throw a party to celebrate that the bad times are behind them. Alternatively, make your first solo birthday an excuse for a big party, invite all the people who have been supportive, and look forward to the future.

# Finding a New Relationship

If you start a new relationship too quickly, you risk bringing all the old baggage with you. So consider the following:

## 1. Check if you're really ready

Divorce is never good for self-esteem and someone, anyone, finding you attractive is bound to go to your head. The giddy excitement of new love will also blow away the blues, so lots of divorcees jump into a new relationship on the rebound. 'It was just going to be a bit of fun,' says Maggie, a thirty-one-year-old personal assistant, 'and we did laugh and I began to feel better and relaxed. That's when he thought I was getting too serious too soon and took off. I came back to earth with a jolt and, in fact, felt worse than I had before.'

**Breakthrough tip:** Do not overlook the importance of time alone, as this is a chance to find your own individual identity before becoming half of a couple again. As a rule of thumb, we need one year to get through all the difficult dates alone first. So surround yourself with friends or family on these difficult occasions.

## 2. Don't get stuck on repeat

Many second-time brides and grooms claim to have moved on by marrying someone completely different from their first partner – but actually have only gone for someone who is the opposite. This means that the same issues are still played out – except from a different position. 'My first husband liked to take charge – to the point of forever telling me what to do and making me feel like a little girl,' says Patsy, a twenty-nine-year-old legal secretary, 'so what I really liked about my second husband was that he was very mild and "take it as you find it". Except nothing seemed to get done, so I found myself making all the decisions and nagging him. Anybody would have thought I was his mother!' Unfortunately, Patsy had not learned to negotiate properly and find a relationship where responsibility was split evenly.

**Breakthrough tip:** The type of woman or man that you are attracted to stretches back to your childhood and how you first learned about relationships: watching your mother and father. The issues they struggled with will be the ones that you are trying to solve too. Understanding these patterns is the first step to breaking them.

## 3. Don't look too far down the line

So a year has passed, you are over the worst and back dating again. However, the temptation is to think every new man or new woman is your happy ending. Although this is natural, because it gives us hope that we are not completely useless at relationships, it does not help to fantasise about what breed of dog you will buy together on the second date. 'I always kept the conversation light,' says Jo, thirty-two, divorced for eighteen months, 'but either the men drifted away or became so clingy that it was claustrophobic.' Although Jo was not aware of it, she was giving off signals that were putting the right men off.

**Breakthrough tip:** Remember there are three types of dates: getting-to-know-you dates (first three to five), fun dates (enjoying each other's company) and courting dates. You cannot get to the third type without moving through the first two. Sometimes a fun relationship, where you can relax and enjoy each other's company, can be very healing and positive – even if it does not lead to a serious long-term relationship. So enjoy the moment.

## 4. Work out what belongs to the past and what to the present

When you start a new relationship, be certain that you do not get angry with your new partner about something that belongs in the past and your previous relationship. Particularly when one is tired or under stress, it is easy to read off an old script. 'I felt myself freeze when John, my new husband, came into the kitchen and announced that he was stopping decorating because he needed to go off into town for a few bits and pieces,' says Suzanne, thirty-five and a mother of two. 'I snapped at him and he got huffy and we had a terrible row about my attitude. It was only later when I'd calmed down that I told him how my first husband would use a million excuses – like not having stuff – to slip out of DIY jobs. But John actually did need more paint.'

**Breakthrough tip:** Become aware of the sensations in your body – your heart beating faster or being flushed in the face – so you can spot the warning signs of anger. Next, remember to 'check it out' before flying into a row from the past relationship. For example: 'I'm sensing that you're using this trip as an excuse – is that right or wrong?'

## 5. Don't compare – even
## in your own head

However much you dislike your ex, there will still be things that you particularly liked: his handiness in fixing the dripping tap, her green fingers. Harping on the past can blind you to your new partner's virtues. Also do not compare yourself to your partner's ex either. 'My second husband has a cottage in Provence – of course he'd bought it with his ex – but had kept joint custody,' says Gillian, a forty-three-year-old saleswoman. 'It's great for our combined troop of children, but the holiday was spoilt because he kept mentioning his ex-wife. How she'd liked this restaurant, about the time they bought that or did this. All the time, I kept thinking, 'Is my cooking up to standard?', 'Did she look better in a bikini?' Although your new partner will have a natural curiosity about the past, after the first twelve months, don't mention the ex (even in a derogatory way).

**Breakthrough tip:** Make friends with other couples who have no memory of either of your first spouses. Adopting, exclusively, each other's old circle of friends can trap the relationship in the past.

# 6. Allow yourself to be vulnerable again

After being hurt, it is natural to hold something back for fear of being devastated again. However, this can also mean that you are not 100 per cent committed to the new relationship or, alternatively, your new partner might feel that he or she doesn't really know you. 'A month after the honeymoon, I was in a really strange mood – caged liked an animal,' says Donna, a twenty-six-year-old fitness instructor. 'My husband asked me what was the matter and I was about to push him away with, "Nothing." Instead a small voice said: "I'm frightened." He came over and held me and I cried and cried. At that moment, I'd never felt closer to him.'

**Breakthrough tip:** It is impossible to avoid pain; it is part of what makes us human. It is better to accept the ups and downs, than take no risks and live life in neutral.

# 7. Believe in yourself

If you have gained more self-knowledge, and in particular a greater understanding of your needs, there is no reason why your new relationship should be anything but a great success. 'When I walked into the registry office, there were so many friends and family from my first grand wedding,' says Lucy, thirty-one. 'I was fearful they were thinking: here we go again. But deep down I knew this time it was really different.'

**Breakthrough tip:** Surround yourself with people who believe in the power of good relationships – rather than friends who run down potential partners. Ultimately we make good choices and with love, and constructive arguing skills, any obstacle can be overcome.

## Summing Up

During a major setback, like a relationship breakdown, it feels like the end of the world. However, the dark days could be the springboard for a new exciting life. The secret is to turn today's bitter lemons into tomorrow's lemonade. With time, self-knowledge and a commitment not to take short cuts, you will reach a better future and fly high again.

**NUTSHELLS FOR LEAVERS:**

- In order to have had the strength to leave, you needed high hopes for the future. Be wary of expecting too much and turning reality into a let-down.
- It is natural to worry sometimes if you have made the right choice. It will pass.
- Remember the courage it took to leave and draw on this resource to keep moving forward.

**NUTSHELLS FOR STICKERS:**

- At the end of the journey, you can accept that your partner had a point when she or he said: 'We'd be better off separating.'
- You have started to embrace the pleasures of being single again.
- The skills learned on the journey, and your commitment to making relationships work, mean that you will find love second time round.

# FINAL NUTSHELLS

## 1. Make a Good Ending

- How you separate will affect your prospects for happiness over the next few years.
- If you are getting divorced, try to keep it as civilised as possible – without guiltily giving your rights away, taking flight to get it over and done with, or dragging it out for sadistic or masochistic reasons.
- If you find yourself fighting for 'a matter of principle' – it is normally a sign that you are trying to punish your ex-partner or are looking for the courts to prove your 'goodness' and your ex-partner's 'badness'. This is nearly always a dead-end and only increases the pain.

- Perhaps you feel hurt and believe that you need redress. In twenty-five years of working with relationships in crisis, I have yet to meet a couple with a wholly innocent or a wholly guilty party. Generally the problem is 'six of one and half a dozen of the other'. If you feel more sinned against than sinning and there-fore 'justified' in punishing your ex-partner, be aware that he or she will only see this bad behaviour (because your ex will have either discounted or forgotten all the contributing factors) and feel, in turn, justified to strike back. Without knowing it, you have reached a negative tipping point and bitterness will overwhelm not only your dealings with your ex-partner but everybody else you meet.
- Bitterness is one of the least attractive human emotions, along with contempt and venge-fulness. It repels rather than attracts possible future partners.

**Checkpoint:** Think back over the past week. What kind act have you made towards your ex-partner? If you can think of nothing, look back over the past month. If you still draw a blank, what small act of kindness could you perform? Don't worry, it only has to be small – like forwarding on his or her post.

# 2. Resolve and Contain
# New Arguments

- When you have children, there are a multitude of day-to-day issues to resolve. Even couples who only have to unravel their financial affairs find plenty of potential disputes.
- Try to be as rational as possible during disputes, as racking up the anger can bring unbidden flashbacks or refuel past hurts and keep you bound into the old relationship.
- An act of generosity will not only help you move on but also encourage your partner to respond in a similar manner. In this way, you will reach a positive tipping point and it gets easier to contain your feelings; being civilised becomes easier too.

**Checkpoint:** Arguments are easier to resolve if you deal with one issue at a time. To stop yourself moving on to another problem, before resolving the first, put an elastic band round your wrist. When you are on the phone to your ex-partner and feel the temptation to say '... and another thing', ping the band. The small moment of pain will distract you for long enough to break the habit. Afterwards, make a note of your issue and think of bringing it up another time. Often, however, it is not really that important.

# 3. Mourn the Loss

- When we are in pain, it is natural to want to move on as quickly as possible but that is not possible if you are still angry.
- So how do you get rid of the anger – especially if fighting with the ex-partner, revenge and getting even will increase rather than decrease it?
- Don't be afraid to cry. Tears reduce anger significantly and even in the most destructive relationship you can cry for the lost dreams and hopes for the future.
- Craving and mourning can easily be mistaken for each other. Thinking a lot about your ex doesn't automatically mean that they were the 'one' and that you will never recover. More likely, you are slowly processing what happened, understanding your regrets and beginning to heal.
- Unfortunately, some people don't allow themselves to mourn and remain tied into an old relationship – either fantasising about the moment that their ex sees the light and

returns, or becoming a voyeur in his or her new life by using the children as spies.

**Checkpoint:** Ask a trusted friend for a second opinion on how well you are mourning the loss of your relationship. Explain that you want a truthful rather than a cheerleading response. It's nice to hear: 'You're doing wonderfully' but it is ultimately a dead-end. If you feel stuck, discuss with your friend: 'What are the benefits of me staying where I am?' There must be a hidden benefit – or why would you be doing it? (Generally, it is to avoid pain or out of fear.) Finally, ask your friend to spot any behaviour that might be keeping you trapped.

## 4. Rediscover yourself

- At the beginning of a relationship, a couple have to transform themselves from two separate individuals into one partnership.
- To this end, couples pool their talents and one partner, for example, cooks while the other fixes things around the house. On a deeper level, one person might look at a problem rationally while the other looks at the emotions.
- This team-building means that we invest our partner with special talents: 'You are good with

money' or 'You are brilliant at solving disputes between the kids.' Often we deliberately forget some skills – in order to make our partner feel wanted or special – or lose them through neglect.

- Now, your task is to unpick that bond and remember the talents that have lain dormant over the relationship.

**Checkpoint:** Think back to your life before your relationship: What were your interests? What were your ambitions? What did you have to give up because there was not enough time or because your ex-partner actively discouraged it? Then, remembering the old you, imagine introducing him or her to yourself: What would the old you recognise about your life today? What would the old you be surprised about? What would the old you applaud? What would upset him or her?

## 5. Venturing Forth Again

- Often people lose confidence in their judgement after divorce or a relationship breakdown: 'How could I have been so stupid . . .?'
- If this is you, plan just for the short or medium term. Worrying about the future will

overwhelm and frighten you. For the time being, it can look after itself.

- If you are worried about flying solo on social occasions, start with places that are not couple-orientated. For example, learning a new skill at an adult education centre.

**Checkpoint:** Ending a relationship is sad but it offers new adventures. Instead of being depressed about the blank spaces in your diary – that used to be filled by couple time – look at the opportunity of doing something new. The future is out there waiting for you. This is your chance, embrace it.

## FINAL NUTSHELLS FOR BOTH LEAVERS AND STICKERS:

- It does not matter which side of the splitting-up divide that you started, the destination is still recovery.
- Change might not be popular but there is an upside to 'nothing lasts for ever.' It not only guarantees that all pain will pass, but also makes the fleeting golden moment that little bit sweeter.
- Change brings with it new opportunities, new adventures and opens new doors.

# A Note on the Author

Andrew G. Marshall is a marital therapist and the author of *I Love You But I'm Not In Love With You: Seven Steps to Saving Your Relationship*, *The Single Trap: The Two-step Guide to Escaping It and Finding Lasting Love* and *How Can I Ever Trust You Again?: Infidelity: From Discovery to Recovery in Seven Steps*. He writes for *The Times*, the *Mail on Sunday*, the *Guardian*, *Psychologies* and women's magazines around the world. His work has been translated into over fifteen languages. Andrew trained with RELATE and has a private practice offering counselling, workshops, training days and inspirational talks.

www.andrewgmarshall.com